YORK NOTES

Selected Poems from *Opened Ground*

Seamus Heaney

Note by Alasdair Macrae

 Longman　　　　　　　. ress

The Publishers would like to thank Faber and Faber Ltd for their kind permission
to reproduce material from *Opened Ground* by Seamus Heaney

The right of Alasdair Macrae to be identified as Author of this Work has been
asserted by him in accordance with the Copyright, Designs and Patents Act 1988

YORK PRESS
322 Old Brompton Road, London SW5 9JH

PEARSON EDUCATION LIMITED
Edinburgh Gate, Harlow,
Essex CM20 2JE, United Kingdom
Associated companies, branches and representatives throughout the world

© Librairie du Liban *Publishers* and Pearson Education Limited 2000

First published 2000
Second impression 2000

ISBN 0-582-32931-0

Designed by Vicki Pacey
Phototypeset by Gem Graphics, Trenance, Mawgan Porth, Cornwall
Colour reproduction and film output by Spectrum Colour
Produced by Pearson Education China Limited, Hong Kong

CONTENTS

PART ONE

INTRODUCTION   How to Study a Poem   5
                 Reading Seamus Heaney's Poetry   6

PART TWO

COMMENTARIES
                 Note on the Text   8
                 Detailed Summaries   8
                 From *Death of a Naturalist*   8
                     Digging   8
                     Death of a Naturalist   10
                     Personal Helicon   12
                 From *Door into the Dark*   13
                     Requiem for the Croppies   13
                     Bogland   14
                 From *Wintering Out*   16
                     Anahorish   16
                     The Other Side   17
                     The Tollund Man   18
                 From *North*   20
                     Punishment   20
                     Singing School: A Constable Calls   23
                 From *Field Work*   25
                     The Toome Road   25
                     Casualty   26
                     The Skunk   28
                     The Harvest Bow   29
                 From *Station Island*   31
                     Sloe Gin   31
                     Chekhov on Sakhalin   32
                     Sandstone Keepsake   34
                     A Kite for Michael and Christopher   36
                     Station Island   37
                     In the Beech   43
                 From *The Haw Lantern*   44
                     From the Frontier of Writing   44
                     Clearances   46
                 From *Seeing Things*   48
                     The Settle Bed   48

Glanmore Revisted   50
Lightenings – VIII   51
From *The Spirit Level*   52
A Sofa in the Forties   52
St Kevin and the Blackbird   54
'Poet's Chair'   55

PART THREE

CRITICAL APPROACHES

Themes   58
    Fidelity to Places and People of his
        Upbringing   58
    Childhood   60
    Celebration   62
    History   63
    Morality and Politics   64
Techniques   69
    Verse   69
    Language   71

PART FOUR

EXTENDED COMMENTARIES

Poem 1 - Sunlight   73
Poem 2 - The First Flight   76
Poem 3 - Postscript   80

PART FIVE

BACKGROUND

Seamus Heaney   84
Historical Background   85
Literary Background   87

PART SIX

CRITICAL HISTORY AND FURTHER READING

Poetry as Poetry   91
Sociological and Political Readings   92
Further Reading   94

Chronology   97
Literary Terms   104
Author of this Note   106

PART ONE

INTRODUCTION

HOW TO STUDY A POEM

Studying on your own requires self-discipline and a carefully thought-out work plan in order to be effective.

- Poetry is the most challenging kind of literary writing. In your first reading you may well not understand what the poem is about. Don't jump too swiftly to any conclusions about the poem's meaning.
- Read the poem many times, and including out loud. After the second or third reading, write down any features you find interesting or unusual.
- What is the poem's tone of voice? What is the poem's mood?
- Does the poem have an argument? Is it descriptive?
- Is the poet writing in his or her own voice? Might he or she be using a persona or mask?
- Is there anything special about the kind of language the poet has chosen? Which words stand out? Why?
- What elements are repeated? Consider alliteration, assonance, rhyme, rhythm, metaphor and ideas.
- What might the poem's images suggest or symbolise?
- What might be significant about the way the poem is arranged in lines? Is there a regular pattern of lines? Does the grammar coincide with the ending of the lines or does it 'run over'? What is the effect of this?
- Do not consider the poem in isolation. Can you compare and contrast the poem with any other work by the same poet or with any other poem that deals with the same theme?
- What do you think the poem is about?
- Every argument you make about the poem must be backed up with details and quotations that explore its language and organisation.
- Always express your ideas in your own words.

This York Note offers an introduction to the poetry of *Opened Ground* and cannot substitute for close reading of the text and the study of secondary sources.

From the publication of his first collection, *Death of a Naturalist*, in 1966, Seamus Heaney has enjoyed a success remarkable in modern poetry. Since about 1975 he has been the most sought-after poet in the English-speaking world. For anyone at all interested in poetry he has become a measure of quality in contemporary literature and an exemplar of what poetry should be concerned with. His appeal is based, in the main, on three elements: first, a natural talent which he has developed; second, his situation as a poet from Northern Ireland during the past violent generation; and third, his gifts as a public presenter of poetry. Each of these elements and, indeed, his whole appeal, has been questioned by some critics. Popularity is not a common condition of modern poets and Seamus Heaney's popularity has aroused suspicions in some minds. Nonetheless, Seamus Heaney has proved to many that poetry can engage with the most vexing issues, can explore the ranges of the imagination, and can give immense challenge and satisfaction to many people.

There is a humaneness, a fundamental decency in his work, an exultation in ordinary things and activities, a relish in people and a recognition that poetry is a profoundly serious enterprise but not necessarily a pompous or obscure one. The scope of subject and variety of treatment across his work allow even the modestly interested reader to find something of pleasure. There are simple poems and extremely difficult poems. This Note will try to show something of the range of Seamus Heaney's work, to open out the workings of some poems, and investigate the poetic success, or otherwise, of his effort.

Several poems from each of his collections have been chosen for detailed consideration in Part Two (Commentaries) and three poems are analysed more closely in Part Four (Extended Commentaries). Different aspects of Seamus Heaney's mind are revealed in this choice of poems and developments in his craft can be traced across his writing career to date. Many of these poems have been frequently anthologised because they have been recognised as typical representatives of Seamus Heaney's work. The richness of verbal patterning in the poems is aurally satisfying for many readers, and anyone studying a poem by Seamus Heaney should begin by reading the poem aloud and allowing the shape and feel of the patterning to make itself apparent through the ear. In his lecture,

'Feeling into Words' (1974), Seamus Heaney speaks of the sensation of recognising a poem as true or right:

> You hear something in another writer's sounds that flows in through your ear and enters the echo-chamber of your head and delights your whole nervous system in such a way that your reaction will be, "Ah, I wish I had said that, in that particular way." This other writer, in fact, has spoken something essential to you, something you recognise instinctively as a true sounding of aspects of yourself and your experience.

(Preoccupations, p. 44)

COMMENTARIES

Seamus Heaney's individual collections are listed in the section Further Reading. Over the years, three selections of his poems have been published. For the most part, the texts of poems have remained unchanged. There are a few exceptions and, where relevant in these Notes, I have drawn attention to the alteration. The text used in these Notes is the most recent selection: *Opened Ground, Poems 1966–1996* (Faber and Faber, 1998). Some poems have been referred to that are not in this selection and, in these cases, the selection in which they can be found has been indicated.

FROM DEATH OF A NATURALIST (1966)

DIGGING   **The poem explores continuities and discontinuities, comparisons and contrasts, between the poet's work and the work of his father and grandfather**

This, the opening poem in his first collection, *Death of a Naturalist*, and in the different editions of his *Selected Poems*, has come to be seen as a declaration of intent, a statement of position by Seamus Heaney. Written in 1964, it is the first poem where, according to the poet, 'I felt I had done more than make an arrangement of words: I felt that I had let down a shaft into real life'. In a lecture, 'Feeling into Words', delivered in 1974 and published in *Preoccupations*, he offers a substantial commentary on the poem. His father and grandfather made their living on the land and the emblem chosen in the poem for their work is digging with a spade: digging in cultivation and digging out peat for fuel. What Seamus Heaney describes is their expertise with their implement, caught in such terms as 'clean', 'rhythm', 'levered firmly', 'Nicking and slicing neatly' and in the outbursts of admiration, 'By God, the old man could handle a spade. / Just like his old man' and 'I've no spade to follow men like them'. The sounds and shapes of different diggings are conveyed exactly and vividly, and various textures are made tactile in the choice of language: 'rasping ... gravelly ground', 'cool hardness', 'squelch and slap / Of soggy peat'. The progress of the poem is largely associative, one thing reminds him of another, and the **verse** is based loosely on a five-**stress** line, moving freely with shorter and longer lines. The opening two sections are juxtaposed with each other; each has a **rhyme** sound holding it together and each centres on a person (Seamus Heaney and his father).

The activities described are utterly different: writing (or preparing to write) and digging. Looking down at his father, Seamus Heaney is reminded of seeing him when he (Seamus Heaney) was a child and he remembers in intimate detail how his father dug up the new potatoes and how the children gathered them up. And he remembers his grandfather digging out the brick-shaped peats from the bog with methodical industry. The digging activities of the father and grandfather come together in the sensations of the penultimate section and the digging has become confirmed as **metaphorical**, as something inside the poet: 'cuts ... Through living roots awaken in my head'. The poem returns to its opening and the poet's pen has become an implement equivalent to the spade of his father and grandfather. There is a resolution, a sense that a point of decision has been reached, in the final line. This determination replaces the rather comfortable, boyishly boasting tone of 'snug as a gun' with its easy **assonance**. However, underlying the phrase is an echo of 'the pen is stronger than the sword' even if the seriousness of such an echo is undermined by lesser echoes of 'snug as a bug' and 'son of a gun'. Too much can be read into this early poem but Seamus Heaney does align himself and his poetry with useful activities and his later poetry shows much digging into various roots and soils. For Seamus Heaney, poetry is an exploration and a revelation. Some critics have claimed that, in the poem, he is offering an apology because he does not continue the work and culture of his father and grandfather; the poet does applaud their skilled labour and does acknowledge that he cannot emulate them in that labour but he has his way of living, his way of digging.

> **squat** Seamus Heaney is describing a fountain pen
> **drills** rows or furrows in which potatoes are grown
> **lug** the top edge of the blade of the spade
> **rooted ... tops** removed the potato plants, the foliage

turf peat cut and dried for fuel

mould could be the soil turned over in the digging or it could be the rotted old potato out of which the new potatoes have grown

DEATH OF A NATURALIST

A child's curiosity about the natural world and the fears based on ignorance and imagination are investigated

The poem is in two parts: the first describes a childhood environment; the second describes a particular day, a particular incident and focuses more on the narrator. The lines are all much the same length with varying patterns of stress and only a quarter of the lines end with a punctuation mark, allowing the narrative to move easily, unmechanically. In the language, there are shifts from sophisticated, adult perceptions as in the opening six lines to a childlike voice as in the final six lines of the first section. Throughout, there is an emphasis on thick, heavy textures with a decided undertone of unpleasantness: 'festered', 'rotted', 'sods', 'sweltered', 'slobber', 'frogspawn', 'clotted', 'jellied', 'rank', 'cowdung', 'air was thick', 'gross-bellied', 'slap and plop', 'mud', 'slime'. At the beginning of the poem there are what appear to be strong statements, signposts, but they are not so easy to decipher. First, there is the title, 'Death of a Naturalist'. The naturalist, we presume after reading the poem, is the young Seamus Heaney interested in the processes of nature who received a frightening rebuke to his curiosity. 'Death' might seem a melodramtic word in the context but some innocent, glib acceptance of these processes was terminated. The second statement occurs in the opening: 'All year the flax-dam festered in the heart / Of the townland'. 'Festered' implies that a wound has gone septic and the whole sentence suggests that an infection afflicted the community for an entire year. Is this a boy's exaggeration of his own turmoil or is Seamus Heaney indicating a larger dimension of unease inside which the boy's experience takes place? The rotting down of the flax and loosening of the fibres is emblematic of a wider loosening and transformation. There is something exaggerated and even exotic in the intense activity of the dam: the bubbles of gas make a gentle muttering noise ('gargled delicately') in contrast to the hectic buzzing of the bluebottles whose intersecting noisy flights make a mesh ('gauze') above the pool and dragon-flies and bright butterflies add colour and shapes. Seamus Heaney's concentration, however, is on the frogspawn. Gathering the spawn in jars, observing each change day by day from spawn to wriggling tadpoles to small frogs, these are experiences shared by so many children. This is basic zoology, the jampot as laboratory, the child feeling responsible for bringing something to life.

In the second section the mood changes, and the simple explanations of Miss Walls, the teacher, cannot cope with the brutal and terrifying happenings. The earlier hints of something unsavoury in 'festered', 'rotted' and 'punishing' now emerge openly; the domesticated 'daddy frog' and 'mammy frog' are forgotten as the 'angry frogs / Invaded the flax-dam'. The delicate gargling of the bubbles and the gauze of the bluebottles is replaced by the 'coarse croaking' of the frogs who have taken possession of their territory. The earlier delicacies and human interferences are repulsed by the vulgar power of the frogs with their 'obscene threats' and 'farting'. The notion of threat is amplified in 'cocked' (like a gun ready to be fired), 'pulsed' (as if to take off), 'poised like mud grenades' (set to explode). The child realises that he has taken liberties and that nature can retaliate and insist on its powers: 'the great slime kings' are in control of their territory and could even move in pursuit of the intruder. The poem, reminiscent of passages in Wordsworth, explores an overlap particularly in our childhoods, but not at all exclusively so, of innocence and a sense of guilt, of intrusion on mysteries we do not understand. More specifically, our understanding or lack of understanding of sexuality is exposed. The teacher tries to offer an explanation of daddy and mammy and eggs which will quieten the child's curiosity. The actuality is cruder and often very shocking.

flax-dam dammed pool in which cut flax plants could be soaked as part of the process of making linen. Linen making was common in Northern Ireland

townland township or small rural community

gauze thin, loosely woven material, often used as a dressing on wounds

slobber wet and slimey substance

gross-bellied with swollen, repulsive bellies

cocked erect or in a state of readiness (as a gun set to fire)

PERSONAL HELICON

> Another poem looking back to Seamus Heaney's
> childhood, this relates his liking for wells as a child with
> his writing of poems as an adult. The poem is dedicated to
> Michael Longley, a fellow poet in Northern Ireland

The five stanzas have the same verse form. In each, the even lines rhyme
with each other as do the odd lines but the odd-line rhymes are more
straightforward or complete than the even-line rhymes. The lines are
similar in length syllabically but there is no fixed pattern to the stresses.
The effect of the form is of tidy regularity but without constraint.
Equally, the shape of thought in the poem is simple: four stanzas recall
experiences of childhood and the final one brings his taste for wells into
the present. Different wells provided different pleasures to the senses,
sounds, smells, sights, and always there was an element of daring in
investigating them. Something secret was unveiled, a mystery was
explored, the unexpected was confronted even when it was frightening.
The boy's relish is apparent in the details of description and
emphasised in the explicit declarations of 'loved', 'savoured', 'fructified'.
In exploring the different wells, the young Seamus Heaney was exploring
aspects of himself, his enjoyments and his fears. The series of itemised
memories, often in short statements like entries in a notebook, leads out
of the past tense into the present tense of the final stanza when Seamus
Heaney takes stock of his current activity. Actual wells and memories of
them fed into his idea of inspiration. The title of the poem now comes
into play and the connection between his childhood interest in wells and
his adult poetry, his personal Helicon, becomes clear. 'Helicon' is a term
for poetic inspiration (see note below) and poetry has replaced and
exploited the earlier wells as a source of pleasure and a means of
authenticating something in himself. In a tone of mild self-mockery he
explains that he is no longer permitted to engage in childish games: it 'is
beneath all adult dignity'. However, in invoking Narcissus, even to mock
the notion, he perhaps concedes that writing poetry may be an acceptable
mode in an adult world of peering at oneself and engaging in some self-
regard. He still enjoys daring the darkness and making it echo with his
activity.

Helicon in Classical Greece it was a mountain, home to the poetic Muses. Poetic inspiration was deemed to derive from two sacred fountains or wells on the mountain and, over the centuries, the name Helicon came to be used as the source or well of inspiration

ditch Irish form of dyke, a low stone wall

Fructified made fruitful

mulch half-rotted plant material

scaresome scary (compare 'fearsome')

Narcissus in Greek mythology, a beautiful youth who fell in love with his own reflection in a pool and drowned; a term for someone who is full of self-regard

echoing perhaps a reference to Echo who, in the myth, fell in love with Narcissus but when her love was not returned she faded away until only her voice remained

FROM DOOR INTO THE DARK (1969)

REQUIEM FOR THE CROPPIES

> Written in the collective voice of the croppies (see below) killed at the battle of Vinegar Hill, the poem commemorates their struggle and suggests that something has grown out of their sacrifice

In 1966 many Irish poets felt impelled to write to commemorate the fiftieth anniversary of the Easter Rising of 1916 (see Historical Background). Seamus Heaney felt (see *Preoccupations*, p. 56) that the seeds of the Easter Rising had been sown in the events of 1798 and in the poem he uses this image of seed growing. The croppy army travelled light and survived on a meagre diet of barley. When they were buried in mass graves, the barley in their pockets sprouted and grew again through the soil. The croppies were mainly rural workers, not regular soldiers, relied heavily on guerrilla tactics, and were crudely armed, often only with farm implements. In form, the poem is a rough sonnet in two rhyming quatrains and a sestet. The rhymes are sometimes obvious, sometimes blurred. The syntax is unelaborate and each line can be read as a unit as if each item is blurted out. The poem reads like a translation and, indeed, the croppies in 1798 would have probably spoken Irish not

English. Their opponents are given no solid identity but they have
infantry, cavalry and cannon and have no respect for the dead
croppies. The croppies are fighting for their land, 'in our own country',
and their uprising is communal, including the priest and the tramp.
Behind the poem lies a repetition of bloody events in the struggle by
Irish people to own and manage their own country. The notion of
blood sacrifice and martyrdom is central to the awareness of the past
in Ireland and dominates present consciousness; the dead are still
alive.

Requiem (Latin) rest; opening word of the mass for the dead; used of a song
lamenting or commemorating the dead

Croppies in the national discontent against the English authorities and
ownership of land in Ireland at the end of the eighteenth century, the
croppies were ordinary men from rural communities who organised
themselves into an irregular army sometimes commanded by priests. After
some military successes they were finally defeated with huge slaughter by
regular troops at Vinegar Hill in County Wexford on 21 June 1798. Novels,
poems, songs and paintings have made the 'croppy boy' into a figure of the
nationalist rebel and martyr

striking dismantling a campsite

on the hike describes the amateur, impromptu nature of the croppy
band

conclave assembly (ironically used because 'conclave' usually describes a
friendly meeting of church leaders)

Terraced in ranked lines, like lines of terracing on a hillside

BOGLAND   **A contrast is drawn between the wide expanse of prairies
in North America and the narrowly bounded landscape
of the bogs in Ireland. Exploration in Ireland can move
only downward. The poem is dedicated to T.P.
Flanagan, a landscape painter with whom Seamus
Heaney spent a holiday in Donegal in 1968 when the
poem was written**

'Bogland', the final poem in Seamus Heaney's second collection, _Door
into the Dark_, is a justification of his choice of Ireland as his poetic
territory. Critics have sometimes criticised his poems for being too local

but he uses the image of the bog to argue that depth rather than extent is just as rewarding. Large areas of Ireland, particularly the centre, consist of deep peat bogs. This is the first poem in which Seamus Heaney uses one of his recurring images of the bog as a repository or museum of the island's past. For his painter friend, T.P. Flanagan, the bog landscape was a place of visual delight and an inspiration for his painting. For Seamus Heaney, the main excitement comes from the archaeological and metaphorical richness: the levels of peat show the layers of Irish life and previous settlement. Peat as a substance acts as a preservative; hence, the skeleton of the elk, the butter and the relics of earlier cultures. (The museums in Ireland are full of objects found in the peat bogs.) The imagery conveys an ambivalence as well as a defensive attitude towards this territory. The horizon on the small island is always 'Encroaching' and 'the cyclops' eye' does not sound entirely friendly. The final line has a menace as well as an excitement; children were often warned that there are holes in the bog which go down for ever. At the same time, the 'ground itself is kind, black butter' and this comfortable image counteracts the earlier unyielding 'crusting' and the later soggy 'soft as pulp'. Ireland does not have the vast open spaces of America but its history is more obvious; the peat is too recent 'By millions of years' to change into coal but it holds the story of the country. Seamus Heaney, in his use of 'we' and 'our' identifies himself with this story.

> **Bogland** soggy peat formed by decomposed vegetation; jocular description of Ireland
> **cyclops** in Greek mythology a giant with one large eye in the middle of its forehead
> **tarn** small lake in mountains or moorland
> **sights** as if the sun is taking aim with its rays and heat
> **Great Irish Elk** large deer of the moose family, long extinct in Ireland
> **definition** transformation (into coal)
> **pioneers** explorers like the early settlers in America (literally diggers)
> **seepage** as if the Atlantic welled up through the deep holes in the bog

FROM WINTERING OUT (1972)

ANAHORISH   Decoding a place name provides an insight into the past life of a locality and its significance for its inhabitants

Wintering Out, the collection in which this poem appeared, contains several examples of a tradition in Irish poetry known as **dinnshenchas** in which the linguistic elements and lore of a place name are explored. It is a kind of praise poetry, a way of understanding one's locality. Other poems in *Wintering Out* in this genre include 'Gifts of Rain', 'Toome', 'Broagh' and 'A New Song'; they all feature places around where Seamus Heaney was born. In the opening line he translates literally the Irish name 'Anahorish' and then moves associatively from there. The 'place of clear water' suggests pure beginnings, a welling-up to spill across the landscape. The sounds of the syllables combine with the sense elements to convey shapes and textures of land: 'soft gradient / of consonant, vowel-meadow' and the reflected light reminds him of lamps carried in the farmyard in his childhood. Memory moves into imagination as he translates the people of his time going about their farm chores into earlier inhabitants, the 'mound-dwellers', dimly perceived. The place with its name remains and each new generation of inhabitants repeats a human settlement in the place. Time dissolves in the 'place of clear water' but, paradoxically, the past is preserved as if in ice.

> **Anahorish** corruption of Irish anach fhior uisce; 'fior' has the sense of 'true' or 'pure'
> **lane** the narrow route found by the running water
> **mound-dwellers** people in neolithic times who built mounds of earth and stone
> **wells and dunghills** two contrasting but essential features of settled habitation

THE OTHER SIDE

Concerned with divisions and neighbourliness, the poem looks back to the sectarian situation of his early life and wonders if communication between such different people is possible

Apart from the brief portrait of a Presbyterian in 'Docker' in *Death of a Naturalist*, this is the first published poem in which Seamus Heaney faces the religious divisions in Northern Ireland. The title introduces a notion of distinctions and possibly opposition. A stream divides the Heaneys' farm, from that of their neighbour; they are Catholic, he is Presbyterian. A mixture of attitudes emerges in how Seamus Heaney describes the situation. The Heaneys' land seems unproductive: 'It's poor as Lazarus, that ground', it has 'moss and rushes', symptoms of poor drainage or neglect and is 'scraggy' and weedy.

In contrast, the neighbour's farm seems lush and fertile: 'his lea [grassy meadow] sloped / to meet our fallow', the 'promised furrows' have a hint of the biblical Promised Land flowing with milk and honey, and the **simile**, 'like loads of hay / too big for our small lanes' emphasises the difference in wealth. The neighbour's speech is dense with quotations and examples taken from the Bible, the 'Book' in section II, and some of this biblical speech seems to rub off on the poet as in 'vouching' and 'tares'. A judgemental and self-righteous attitude is attributed to the neighbour in sections I and II in his 'biblical dismissal' of the Heaneys' efforts and his 'patriarchal dictum'. His life is organised, doctrinaire and rather bleak: consider the final stanza of section II. In the third section a more sympathetic view is offered where Seamus Heaney understands the neighbour's awkwardness and his clumsy attempts to be neighbourly. Behind the poem lies the enquiry by Jesus (Luke 10) into 'Who is my neighbour?' but it is significant that the biblical references attributed to the Presbyterian are mainly from the more austere Old Testament. The saying of the Catholic rosary at their evening prayers by the Heaney family is as exotic and mysterious to their neighbour as is his recitation of biblical names and texts to them. The final ten lines of the poem are in the present tense as if Seamus Heaney has grown up or moved into his imagination and his own awkwardness matches that of his neighbour. In many respects the Heaneys and their neighbour have much in common;

the poem is not about hostility but, rather, difference, suspicion and ignorance. The unrhymed three-line units give a sense of ordering but the unmechanical **stress** pattern emphasises a freedom of movement, a sense of thinking and feeling.

vouching declaring (old-fashioned, biblical)

Lazarus emblem of a poor man (see Luke 16)

Tongue ... people language of the Jews, the chosen people, in the Old Testament of the Bible. Also a suggestion of the Elect in Calvinist theology, people favoured by God

blackthorn farmer's stick

prophesied pronounced judgement like the prophets in the Old Testament

pollen 'male', fertilizing powder in plants (Seamus Heaney seems to use the word as if it means the seed of the weeds)

tares weeds (biblical)

rehearse repeat with mockery

patriarchal dictum categorical statement made by the authoritative figures in the Old Testament

Lazarus ... Goliath figures from the Bible used as examples

Your ... house Catholics in the community

body ... kirk space for the congregation in a church, specially Presbyterian and unadorned (note the colloquialism)

rosary string of beads used in the Catholic Church to help in the recitation of set prayers

litany recitation of the prayers

right-looking it seems to be good weather

dandering strolling casually (he wishes to give the impression that he has not called with any purpose)

party present but out of place

THE TOLLUND MAN

Seamus Heaney contemplates a photograph of the preserved body of a man from Tollund and traces parallels between the imagined situation of the dead man and the poet's own time in Northern Ireland

In his lecture, 'Feeling into Words', published in *Preoccupations*, Seamus Heaney describes how this poem came into being. He relates how he was inspired by P.V. Glob's *The Bog People* (translated 1969) which attempts to explain the significance of bodies dating from the early centuries AD found in the bogs of Jutland in Denmark. The extraordinarily preserved head from the body of a man dug up at Tollund is now on display in the Silkeborg Museum near Aarhus. Professor Glob advances the theory that the man was sacrificed in a ritual to honour the goddess of fertility and, thereby, ensure the success of the next harvest. Thinking about the theory, Seamus Heaney was prompted to compare that sacrifice with the violent deaths of young men in the cause of Ireland, symbolically represented as Mother Ireland or Kathleen Ni Houlihan.

Of the three sections, the first and third are mainly centred on the Tollund Man, the second introduces stories of atrocities from nearer at hand and closer in time. The dominant tenses are past and future, and the present is explicit only in the lines: 'Now his stained face / Reposes at Aarhus'. The narrator's involvement, however, forces our attention to his present situation. In the first section he states his resolution to go to Aarhus; in the third **stanza** he identifies himself with the Man when we are trapped into misreading the lines: 'I will stand a long time. / Bridegroom to the goddess', as if he, the narrator, is the bridegroom (the Man). We are momentarily confused by the regularity of the stanza form to read across the full stop in line 10. In the second section the narrator takes risks and invokes a power from the dead man. In the final section, he implicates himself in the Tollund Man's death by the positioning of 'driving' as if he could be driving the tumbril carrying the condemned victim rather than just driving as a tourist in modern Denmark. This involvement between Seamus Heaney and the Tollund Man is most marked in the paradoxical phrases in the final section: 'sad freedom' and 'I will feel lost, / Unhappy and at home' where he imaginatively enters into the Man's sacrificial death. The poem has moved from this factual description of the body, to the idea of marriage and martyrdom to the goddess, to invocation (as to a saint) for help, to a reconstruction of the Man's final journey, to Seamus Heaney's sense of complicity in the event. The distant (Aarhus) is brought close ('home') and the remote past is aligned with something in the present through the incidents in Ireland described in the second section. Seamus Heaney sees a repeated pattern across time and place, and strives to understand the killings and hopes to see something good emerge from the violence. There is a desperation in his resolve 'I will go', 'I will stand', 'I could risk blasphemy', but at the end there is a bleak pessimism in 'I will feel lost, / Unhappy and at home'. In ancient Jutland the ritual sacrifice had an accepted, holy and beneficent place in the tribe's scheme of things; the killings in Northern Ireland seem random and fruitless.

gruel thin porridge

torc metal band, commonly worn round neck or arm by ancient Celts

fen marsh or wet bog

kept preserved (as if miraculously)

Trove valuable found object

Honeycombed workings the face of the bank from which peat (turf) has been cut. The spade marks look like the cell pattern in a comb of honey

Consecrate declare sacred or worthy of veneration

cauldron in the shape of a basin (Seamus Heaney may have had in mind the richly decorated sacred cauldrons found in the bogs of Jutland)

The scattered ... farmyards victims of sectarian killings in rural Northern Ireland

sleepers heavy wooden beams on which railway lines are laid

four young brothers infamous atrocity against Catholics committed by irregular Government police in the 1920s

tumbril cart used to transport condemned person to execution

Tollund ... Nebelgard places in Jutland

FROM NORTH (1975)

MOSSBAWN: TWO POEMS IN DEDICATION
          I Sunlight

See Poem 1 of Extended Commentaries

PUNISHMENT   **Seamus Heaney again draws a parallel between a preserved body, this time that of a young woman, and events around him in Northern Ireland. He tries to probe his own position in relation to these events**

Like many of the poems in Part I of *North*, 'Punishment' is written in stanzas of four shortish lines without rhyme and usually with two or three main stresses in each line. The feel of the verse is deliberate but not mechanical, meditative but not spacious. The poem consists of two equal halves: in the first, the woman is described; in the second, the woman is addressed, 'she' changes to 'you'. In the second half Seamus Heaney's involvement becomes much more personal marked by an increase in 'I'. This involvement is anticipated in his attempts earlier on to imagine himself into her experience of dying: 'I can feel', 'I can see'. Her vulnerability is stressed in her naked exposure to the cold wind, the 'tug / of the halter', her body being held under the watery bog, and her shaved head. She was blindfolded before being killed and her happy memories were blotted out. Seamus Heaney carries this vulnerable quality through to the second half, particularly in lines 23–7. It would seem that her crime was adultery and according to the rules of her tribe she had to be punished by a particular form of death.

Seamus Heaney is drawn by her attractiveness and by his feeling that she is a victim, that she is punished for showing love. In his mind she becomes a scapegoat for her society's sense of guilt; an example is made of her so that other people do not have to examine their own behaviour. Seamus Heaney runs together the two biblical notions of the scapegoat and the woman brought to Jesus accused of adultery. Although he has built her up to be so appealing ('almost love you'), he concedes that if he had been there when she was judged he would not have had the courage to intervene on her behalf. He would not have been actively involved in her killing but, equally, he would not have disassociated himself from his tribe's punishment of her. Acknowledging the oddities of seeing her dead body aesthetically or even erotically, he is raising a moral question about the detached, observant stance of the poet in relation to actual situations, and, in particular, the painful situations around him in Northern Ireland as described in the final two stanzas. Seamus Heaney is referring to instances where women from the Catholic community had dealings with British soldiers and were brutally humiliated and punished by groups from their own community such as the IRA. His confusion of feeling is emphasised in the tangle of complicated and contradictory terms of the final stanza. The word 'connive' can mean: to pretend ignorance of something one dislikes, or to choose to ignore something one is expected to disapprove of but with which one secretly sympathises, or to act secretly in favour of something one publicly condemns.

Seamus Heaney sets up a rivalry between 'civilised' and 'tribal'; he sees the cruelty, the uncivilised punishment in the treatment of the 'betraying' women but he also feels, because of his whole upbringing and sense of belonging to that community, the justice of the punishment. This dilemma of rival moralities in himself is shared by many people in similar complicated situations. Seamus Heaney has tried, as in 'The Tollund Man', to find a way of making sense of the tribal or sectarian killings in Northern Ireland by relating these contemporary events to killings in a very different kind of community.

It may be that no worthwhile comparison can be established, that circumstances and attitudes may be too dissimilar, that adultery can not be seen as equivalent to non-conformism. Seamus Heaney, however, does not propose solutions or explanations of such a universal nature. Rather, he is provoked by studying Glob's evidence to reconsider his own position as a man and as a poet regarding the brutal events in a community where he is a member and an observer.

halter cord with a noose for leading her

amber yellowish solidified resin from trees used to make ornaments

rigging like the pattern of ropes on a sailing ship on which the sails are suspended (the flesh had gone)

weighing a large boulder was pressing her body down and above it were branches

barked sapling a young tree stripped of its bark and all white

oak-bone when the body was dug up the diggers could not easily distinguish bone from wood

brain-firkin her skull is a small cask holding her brains

tar-black stained by the peat

scapegoat according to the Bible, the high priest of the Hebrews selected a goat and symbolically laid the sins of the tribe on it before driving it out into the desert

stones in St John's gospel, chapter 8, a woman accused of adultery is brought before Jesus and he is asked whether or not she should be punished in the traditional way by being stoned to death. Jesus says: 'He that is without sin among you, let him throw the first stone'

artful clever or crafty, or as an artist

voyeur someone who takes pleasure, particularly sexual, from observing others rather than from active participation

brains ... combs the brains were removed from the skull for examination and the ridges were still intact

webbing network

numbered archaeologists number the items in order so that the body can be moved and reassembled

cauled covered or painted. A caul is the membrane round a foetus in the womb. Seamus Heaney seems to use the word **ironically** in that it suggests innocence and was thought, if it emerged on the head of the new-born child, to protect the person from drowning

tar ... railings commonly the women had their hair shaved off, were stripped, tarred and tied to public railings

S INGING SCHOOL: 2 A CONSTABLE CALLS

'Singing School' is a sequence poem consisting of six sections which reflect on aspects of Seamus Heaney's life and his development as a poet. Section 2 looks back to an incident in his childhood when the local policeman came to check that the poet's father was growing the crops he was entitled to grow

The sequence takes its title from W.B. Yeats's 'Sailing to Byzantium' (1926) and in several of the sections there is an engagement with other writers in a manner new in Seamus Heaney's work. He uses as an epigraph for the sequence lines from Wordsworth's long biographical poem *The Prelude* (1805) beginning: 'Fair seedtime had my soul, and I grew up / Fostered alike by beauty and by fear'. Fear and guilt lie behind the child's attitude presented in 'A Constable Calls'. Furthermore, Seamus Heaney echoes the title of a play by J.B. Priestley, *An Inspector Calls* (1945), in which each of the characters in a house turns out to have something to hide, something each of them feels may be discovered by the police inspector. Although in the poem the constable is engaged in a routine inspection of quotas of crops on the farm, the farmer father plays a very small part and we see the episode entirely through the child's apprehension: 'I assumed / Small guilts and sat / Imagining the black hole in the barracks'. Each ordinary movement of the policeman, each item of his bicycle, is invested with something fearful, almost menacing. The first odd word in the poem is 'relieved' in line 7, odd because it suggests that the inanimate bicycle usually suffers under the 'boot of the law' – a phrase half solemn and half comical. There is an emphasis throughout on measurement, on deliberation, and the boy is afraid in case he or his father does not fit exactly to the requirements: 'Arithmetic and fear'. The small lapse from the regulations in the line of forbidden turnips becomes, in the boy's mind, a crime to be punished, if discovered, with imprisonment in 'the black hole' of the police station. What was alert observation in the first half of the poem becomes much tenser in the final three stanzas. The 'heavy ledger' has become 'the domesday book'; the policeman's cap almost off-duty 'upside down / On the floor' reasserts his authority when he fits it on his head 'with two hands'. And, as if he really knows the boy's secret, the policeman 'looked at me as he said goodbye'. The noises of his departure are curiously loud: 'snapping' and 'ticked, ticked, ticked'. Seamus Heaney has caught an atmosphere of dread and furtiveness not uncommon in children. Whether this atmosphere, domestically presented, reflects on or extends to a wider political situation is doubtful but cannot be discounted.

cowl flap (like a small hood) to prevent water from splashing up on the cyclist

'spud' potato-shaped; the dynamo when engaged with the rim of the rear wheel provides power for the bicycle light

cocked back disengaged

bevel exactly drawn line

tillage returns details of which crops are planted where

acres ... perches (now outmoded) measurements

root crops plants grown for their edible roots (not potatoes)

Mangolds? Marrowstems? vegetables grown for animal fodder

black hole echo of the infamous 'Black Hole of Calcutta' 1746, where over one hundred people were confined and suffocated. The punishment cell in a barracks or police-station is nicknamed the 'Black Hole'

domesday book after the Norman Conquest, a survey of all the lands and values of England was made in 1085. Also a reference to Doomsday when the books of record will be opened and all sinners will be judged

FROM FIELD WORK (1979)

THE TOOME ROAD

The poem describes the military occupation of his home territory and the mixture of helplessness and defiance felt by the poet

The structure of thought in the poem moves from the description of the complacent military presence in the opening four lines to two questions with rather oblique responses. The date of the incident is not given and the first question makes any enquiry concerning the date pointless: 'How long were they approaching...?' Seamus Heaney's use of 'charioteers' later on emphasises a long-term pattern rather than something immediate and new. He is reflecting on different kinds of power: military control, land ownership, giving birth, disposing of the dead. Behind all these forms of power there is, he believes, the authority of the place itself, 'The invisible, untoppled omphalos'. The community has grown used to grim events and has developed its own superstitious ways of trying to avert them (lines 11–13). It is difficult to rouse anybody: 'The whole country [is] sleeping'. Some spirit of the locality, however, guarantees a survival despite the adversity. Like the camouflaged armoured cars, **rhyme** seems to disappear and reappear and so too does the omphalos. The word 'omphalos' comes from the Greek for 'navel' and the famous navel-stone in the innermost shrine at Delphi was seen by the ancient Greeks as the midpoint of the entire world. What constitutes the omphalos of Seamus Heaney's home community remains, but a belief in such a centred force is at the heart of his patriotism and his opposition to British occupation of Northern Ireland. The opening section of his autobiographical essay 'Mossbawn' in *Preoccupations* is called 'Omphalos' and in it he sees the village pump as the centre of his childhood world.

Toome   Toome is a village near Seamus Heaney's birthplace

warbling   moving with a melodious, carefree sound (**ironic**)

buckrakes   large frames supporting rakes

Silos   large receptacles in which green crops are compressed and stored to be used as fodder for animals

on the latch   left unlocked

THE TOOME ROAD continued

headstones gravestones to mark the dead
0 charioteers the poetic, old fashioned tone presents the armoured cars and the soldiers in a curious light
dormant temporarily not in use

CASUALTY   Seamus Heaney explores the differences and the affinities between himself, a poet, and the fisherman killed 'accidentally' for defying a curfew imposed by the Provisional IRA in Derry after Bloody Sunday

The poem swings about between 'I', 'my' and 'he', 'his' and, although there is a social context of pubs, funerals and 'our tribe', there is a strong emphasis on the solitary, wayward activity of the drinking fisherman and of the poet with his 'other life'. Each of them is a mystery to the other but the poet identifies with elements in the fisherman's activities, particularly towards the end of the poem where fishing and poetry overlap: 'As you find a rhythm / Working you'. Even in the opening paragraph where Seamus Heaney admires a deftness in his acquaintance, he could be describing an aspect of himself as a poet and raising a doubt about it:

> I loved his whole manner,
> Sure-footed but too sly,
> His deadpan sidling tact

This links with the lines about his own behaviour in the second paragraph, and his 'tentative art' is put under scrutiny by the death of this man, the art and the death held together by the colon in line 37. The three sections unobtrusively move forward in time from the habits of the past to the day of the curfew to the funeral to when the poem is written. Inside that general movement the poet's mind drifts back and forwards and the **imagery**, too, often drifts across subjects: the carried coffins in section II 'Seemed to float ... on slow water'; the fisherman 'drank like a fish ... Swimming towards the lure'; the mourners in section III are described as 'Shoaling' and the 'Purring of the hearse' is repeated in the 'dawdling engine' and 'screw purling' of the boat. Across the three sections **rhyme** is present but is less obvious in places as if it too drifts and tightens. It is most apparent in the opening description of habitual, physical activities. In the second and third sections the meaning thickens as the questions arise and Seamus Heaney's attitude becomes more problematic. In section II, lines 9–13 are very complicated. 'Swaddling' is normally associated with newly born babies and protected innocence. 'Lapping' may continue that line of thought but Seamus Heaney is describing a funeral and the swaddling band is unrolled to become 'tightening' and the community is 'braced and bound'. This sense of constriction is intensified and darkened in the line 'Like brothers in a ring' as if something explosive is about to occur. In the final seven lines of section II the crucial question of blame and guilt, of the individual in relation to a community, is asked but not answered. In effect, the question is posed again at the end of the poem. Seamus Heaney's emphasis on the individuality of the fisherman and his obvious delight in the man's trueness to his chosen way of living make it difficult for us not to sympathise with him but the shared grief of the Bogside, the 'packed cathedral', the 'common funeral', 'his own crowd', 'Our tribe's complicity' constitute a massive, rival moral force. Although he is described as a 'breadwinner', he appears as a solitary operator without obvious obligations to others. Seamus Heaney cannot answer the challenge in a categorical way but it seems that the balance swings towards the claim of the individual in the final section when he says 'I tasted freedom with him' and discovers his 'proper haunt / Somewhere, well out, beyond…'. The awkward position of the poet as poet was indicated in the first section: it is easier to discuss factual matters. Finally, the choice of title comments on the poem and its issues. There is an element of the accidental or incidental in 'casualty' that there is not in the term 'hero' or 'martyr' or 'victim'. This specific case (the same root as 'casualty') does not provide sufficient evidence from which to offer a general answer.

dumb-show miming

pulling … top pouring a pint of stout

dole-kept breadwinner he supports a family by receiving government money as an unemployed person

plug lump of tobacco from which he cuts pieces with which to fill his pipe

slug drink, a swallow

politic wary, tactful

PARAS … NIL famous piece of graffiti: the British Paratroopers had shot thirteen people from the Bogside, a Catholic area in Derry, on Bloody Sunday

CASUALTY continued

Surplice and soutane loose garments worn by priests
swaddling band length of narrow cloth wrapped round a new-born baby to restrict its movements
Lapping wrapping round
black flags they were flown to show sympathy with the Nationalist struggle and as a mark of respect for the dead
outfaced confronted and defeated
lure something attractive, a device used to catch fish
Puzzle solve
Shoaling moving in formation as fish do
revenant ghost

THE SKUNK The poet is reminded by a sight of his wife of a lonely time years earlier in California when he eagerly awaited the nightly visit of a skunk

This is a love poem but centred on a strange comparison between his wife and a skunk. The comparison mixes the 'Ordinary' and the 'mysterious' (line 18) of both and rests on an affectionately humorous view of his wife. The opening and closing images of the poem are of tails up: the skunk's in stanza 1, his wife's in stanza 6. Both the beginning and the end are presented surprisingly; the opening line and a half do not lead predictably to 'the skunk's tail', and the 'head-down, tail-up' picture of the poet's wife is decidedly comical and not entirely flattering. The poet's vigilance and sense of anticipation, although we accept that they are directed at the skunk, seem more appropriate if related to his wife: 'Night after night / I expected her like a visitor', 'I began to be as tense as a voyeur', 'And there she was, the intent and glamorous'. The middle of the poem, stanzas 3 and 4, makes clear his loneliness, frustration and separation in spite of, and even emphasised by, his exotic surroundings in California. His wife, in her absence from him, becomes a painful obsession for him and releases a wish to express his love to her. The skunk in her faithful visitations becomes, not a substitute for her, but a means of earthing his emotion. When we read stanza 5 and come to 'skunk' we are shocked, we feel that we have been ambushed into identifying Seamus Heaney's wife with the animal. It is Seamus Heaney himself who has 'Mythologized, demythologized' the animal just as, in the final stanza, he simultaneously exalts and undercuts his wife preparing for bed. From the dramatic opening adverb 'Up' and the extravagant simile of the chasuble to the exactness of 'sootfall' and the final romantic touch of the 'black plunge-line nightdress', the poem is a series of exciting surprises.

> **skunk** small North American animal with black and white striped fur and a bushy tail. (The unpleasant connotations of skunks are, I think, irrelevant to the poem)
> **damasked** patterned (like damask cloth)
> **chasuble** garment worn by priest conducting mass (colour varies according to nature of mass)
> **whinnied** when the thermostat on old refrigerators indicated a degree of coldness, the motor stopped its noise with a final shudder
> **voyeur** secret observer particularly of sexual happenings
> **broaching** piercing in order to release liquid
> **mutated** changed, transformed itself
> **eucalyptus** kind of tree common in California with a very specific scent from its leaves
> **Mythologized, demythologized** given special, magical qualities; made ordinary and natural
> **sootfall** the soft sound of her garments dropped on the floor like the sound of a fall of soot from a chimney into the fireplace
> **plunge-line** with low-cut neckline

THE HARVEST BOW

> The stalks of wheat intertwined into a bow by his father provides the poet with a physical link between himself and his father, the present and the past, nature and art

Although each of the five stanzas consists of three rhyming couplets, the rhymes are unemphatic and the punctuation so commonly carries the ear through the lines that the general effect is of meandering thoughts. The poem moves from the physical to memories and musings, 'Gleaning the unsaid off the palpable'. The timespan extends from the time when the poem is written back across the life of the father, and the tradition of the straw bow stretches much further back to when the 'spirit of the corn' was more actively invoked. There is a casualness, a 'throwaway' element in the bow but also a more ritualistic side, something emblematic in the 'frail device'. It is an object which carries an unspoken message, which speaks for the 'silence', the 'unsaid' and the 'tongue-tied'. As a talisman, it has magical powers and supports a continuity of good fortune from generation to generation, father to son, nature to art: '*The end of art is peace*'. The wheat from which the bow was fashioned 'does not rust' and is 'still warm' with the tradition which it represents. Memories of Seamus Heaney's boyhood are prompted by the bow and he recalls walking with his father, together and yet apart (divided by the break between stanza 3 and stanza 4 and the heavy **stress** on 'You' and 'Me').

There is no explicit communication or dialogue between Seamus Heaney and his father but, as in many other poems, the poet tries to show how a verbal reticence in his community is compensated for by handed-on traditions which carry the communal values. In this instance, the bow contains his elderly father's 'mellowed silence' and this silence is 'knowable' to someone who can read its 'braille' and thereby decipher 'that original townland' implicit in the artefact. It is the communal rather than the individual that is stressed: his father's fingers have learned a skill so thoroughly that they can weave the bow without thinking. All through the poem, communal habits and activities are drawn in as a context and the relations between the community and the natural world are symbolised in the harvest bow, particularly in the final **image** of the 'spirit of the corn' as a rabbit which has eluded capture but has been felt.

harvest bow bow made from the stalks of ripe grain at harvest time. Sometimes given as a love-token, sometimes worn at the harvest fair, sometimes kept in the farmhouse till the following year

implicated included in its nature (originally the word meant 'intertwined')

rust deteriorate, grow dull

corona circle of light

ashplants walking stick cut from ash tree

lapped the spurs polished or sharpened the back claws on fighting cocks

Harked listened, attuned

somnambulant as if walking while asleep

Gleaning gathering carefully (the smallest pieces of the harvest)

palpable what can be handled

old beds old metal bed-ends were commonly used as fencing or gates

lift excitement

flushes rouses animals or birds
townland village community
The end of art is peace the purpose of art is to bring contentment (quotation from
Coventry Patmore, 1823–96, and used several times with approval by W. B. Yeats)
device emblematic design (for example, on a coat of arms)
deal unpainted pine wood
drawn snare loop of thin wire (set to catch an animal) has been activated but the
animal has escaped ('slipped')
burnished polished by rubbing

FROM STATION ISLAND (1984)

SLOE GIN   The poem attempts to catch in words the very individual
qualities of sloe gin

Sloe berries when picked in late autumn from the blackthorn bushes on
which they grow are extremely bitter but when they have been steeped in
gin for some months they impart a distinctive and very pleasant flavour
and colour to the gin. Ordinary gin, which is clear coloured, is flavoured
with juniper berries. The opening **stanza** describes the process by which
sloe gin is made. The two sentences seem to be in the wrong order in that
the gin gathers colour from the dark blue sloes once they are together in
the jar. Ordered as it is, the opening is more dramatic with its seasonal
alteration. By the time the jar is opened, the mixing of sloes and gin has
taken place and the sharp particularity of the smell evokes the blackthorn
bush and fills the pantry. Seamus Heaney is alert to sensuous experience
and gifted at finding a verbal formula which causes us to recognise the
sensation. When he pours the gin from the container it is as if he is
liberating a brightness and anticipating the hot kick of the liquor. The
final **stanza** shifts to the present tense and the toast 'to you' shares his
experience. The berries have swollen in the gin and a trace of their deep
colour stirs and twists like thin smoke in the glass. In the drink there is
still the distinctive, bitter edge of the sloes reliably themselves.

tart pungent, sharp and bitter
Betelgeuse bright star in the constellation Orion
mirled twirled or mingled

CHEKHOV ON SAKHALIN

> The poem describes a journey made by Anton Chekhov to
> the penal colony at Sakhalin in Siberia and investigates
> his motives for making the journey. How can the artist
> accommodate in his or her work the acts of cruelty and
> injustice which are integral parts of society?
>
> The poem is dedicated to Derek Mahon, a fellow poet
> from Northern Ireland. Lines 9–11 in *Opened Ground* are
> different from the original in *Station Island*

A number of poems in *Station Island*, apart from the long title poem, are
concerned with self-interrogation. In this case, Seamus Heaney explores
the situation of Chekhov in Russia in 1890 as in some ways parallel to his
own situation in Ireland in the early 1980s. The opening line announces
the conclusion to a debate in Chekhov's mind, 'So, he would pay his
"debt to medicine"'. The ending of the poem is less certain, a confession
of some failure in his mission. Chekhov had trained as a doctor and felt
that working as a writer had diverted him from a more obvious
humanitarian involvement with suffering. His long journey to Sakhalin
was a way of forcing himself to face the suffering and injustice in Russia.
Creating a tension in the poem are the rival pulls of Moscow and
Sakhalin, freedom and chains. The bulk of the poem is occupied with the
evening of his arrival at Sakhalin and his drinking a bottle of cognac.
Given to him by his literary friends in Moscow, the brandy represents
that world of glamour and sophistication he has left behind and offers
a final treat before he has to confront the harsh actuality of Sakhalin.
The incompatible claims on him coexist awkwardly in the sixth stanza in
the ring of the breaking brandy glass and the ring of the convicts' chains;
also there is an ambiguity in the word 'burden' which can mean a refrain
or chorus and a weight of responsibility. In his family history Chekhov
could see a parallel to his present dilemma. His grandfather had been
a serf, his father had been an unsuccessful storekeeper (see line 13),
and now he was an accepted member of Russia's glittering society.
Chekhov, however, never came to feel totally contented with his social
and literary success; 'His slave's blood' (line 27) could not be easily
removed. In the poem he appreciates the pleasures of his success:

Seamus Heaney describes Chekhov's enjoyment of the cognac with a combination of sacred and profane images, the 'holier joy' (line 16) and the 'pert young cleavage' (line 18). The poet presents him as having made the arduous journey of over 3000 miles and he is reviewing moments from the journey and enjoying his final hours of freedom before he crosses to the prison on the island. The concluding six lines look 'ahead' to the months spent on the island when Chekhov struggles to find a satisfactory way of writing about the horrifying scenes without preaching ('tract') or mere observational documentary ('thesis'). And can he release the guilt instilled in him from his background? Is there a progression towards a more valid freedom from the 'swimming free' (line 4), 'freedom' (line 24) to 'the free man' (line 27)?

At no point in the poem does Seamus Heaney intervene directly. He relates the story and problem of Chekhov with dramatic vividness but without obvious interference. It is from the poem's context in Seamus Heaney's career and in the collection *Station Island* and in relation to the appalling events in Northern Ireland in the early 1980s that we can discern a vital connection between Chekhov's situation and Seamus Heaney's. The artist enjoys certain kinds of freedom and suffers certain varieties of responsibility and guilt. Can the artist ever find 'the right tone' or 'walk away from the floggings'? The persistent off-rhyming throughout the poem points not to a 'right tone' but to a wrong note; and the ambivalences in the imagery of enjoyment and disgust point to an irresolution or continuing struggle.

> **Chekhov** Anton Chekhov (1860–1904), Russian short-story writer and dramatist. Admired for his blend of **pathos** and humour particularly in seeing characters in periods of social change
>
> **Sakhalin** island off the east coast of Siberia, some 3000 miles from Moscow, used as a penal colony for criminals and political prisoners. Chekhov spent the summer of 1890 on the island and wrote a book in 1895 about his experiences there
>
> **cognac** highly regarded brandy from the French area called Cognac. It would have been very expensive and smart in Chekhov's Russia
>
> **ocean** the Pacific
>
> **troikas** Russian carriages drawn by three horses abreast
>
> **Tyumin** town in central Siberia

Lake Baikal large lake in eastern Siberia
literati educated people (seen as a group) interested in writing
cantor singer who leads the singing of music at the mass
iconostasis screen separating the altar from the congregation and often
carrying sacred images
salon social gathering of fashionable or distinguished people in a large
reception room of a grand house
Inviolable and affronting simultaneously untouchable and challenging
midnight sun in the far north in summer the sunlight remains throughout
most of the night (Seamus Heaney seems to have located Sakhalin further
north than it actually is)

SANDSTONE KEEPSAKE

**The poet is reminded by the stone of the evening and
place where he found it and of the thoughts aroused in
him on that occasion**

The poem begins in the present but **stanzas** 2–5 are all in the past tense.
The link between past and present is the lump of sandstone which now
has its own comfortable, physical familiarity for the poet but also
represents a complex of thoughts and feeling experienced on that evening
some time before and obviously still reverberating in the poet's mind. The
ordinariness of the stone, out of its original water, is emphasised in its
feel, 'so reliably dense and bricky'. As often happens, a stone appears
more exciting, more special in the context in which we find it, particularly
with the added colour of wetness. In the second stanza, the associations
later evoked by the stone in Seamus Heaney's mind are intimated or
prepared for by the words 'ruddier' and 'contusion' with their usual
connections, respectively, with human complexion and bruised bodies,
with blood under the skin. The bloodiness is developed in stanzas 3 and
4 in 'bloodied' and the 'heart' taken from the body of Henry (see note).
Even with the early intimation, lines 10–11, the allusion to Phlegathon
comes as a shock; the poem seems to have hit a sudden intensity: 'hell's
hot river'. This new note is strengthened in the following five lines with
his hand smoking as it were from the burning blood of the water and
Seamus Heaney imagining his hand plucking out the heart of the young
Henry. The dash at the end of line 14 breaks this desperate, inflamed way

of thinking and self-accusation, and the poet readjusts himself to his situation: 'Anyhow, there I was'.

The other main element in the poem, referred to almost casually in lines 8–9, now becomes prominent in the fifth stanza. We become aware now that Seamus Heaney's wild imaginings about blood and killing and punishment resulted from a conjunction of the particular stone, the prison camp, atrocities in the society and his own place in relation to these atrocities. **Images** of violence, revenge, martyrdom and guilt jostle in his head but he pulls himself away from these lurid, nightmarish thoughts and asserts, self-deprecatingly, his ordinariness. The shifts of tone are disconcerting to the reader; 'hell's hot river' and the 'victim's heart in his casket, long venerated' do not fit easily with the factual detail of stanza 1 and the 'scarf and waders' in stanza 6. In the end, the poet appears to dismiss himself as beneath official interest, with no ambitions or ideals regarding his society. However, the final word 'venerators' which he applies to himself is too big to be seen as dismissal. It echoes the phrase 'long venerated' in line 16 and asserts, through this echo, that there may be a positive value in remaining not aloof from but outside the violent struggle. Seamus Heaney looks across from the Republic of Ireland, the Free State, to the watch-towers and embattled bitterness of Northern Ireland; he partly mocks his poet's 'free state of image and allusion', demonstrated in the poem, but he also declares where he stands, however difficult and even paradoxical his position may be.

> **Keepsake** something kept as a reminder of someone or some event (more personal than a souvenir)
> **gourd** tropical fruit often pear-shaped. Rind used as a water container when emptied and dried
> **sedimentary** as if the constituent matter had sunk to the bottom, basic
> **Inishowen** on the Irish ('Free State') side of the Foyle estuary. Opposite, in Northern Ireland, is Magilligan, the site of a detention centre for prisoners
> **perimeter** guarded boundary fence
> **Phlegethon** river of burning blood in hell in Greek mythology. Used by Dante in the Hell section (Canto XII) of his *Divine Comedy* as the place of suffering for people who had committed acts of violence against their fellow men

Guy de Montfort English noble who in 1272 avenged the murder of his father by killing his cousin Prince Henry, nephew to King Henry III, at mass in the cathedral at Viterbo in Italy. Dante imagined Guy de Montfort as being eternally punished in Phlegethon for his crime

victim's heart a statue of Prince Henry was supposedly erected in London and showed him carrying a casket containing his heart. Pilgrims came to venerate or revere the heart in the casket as a holy object

A KITE FOR MICHAEL AND CHRISTOPHER

Making and flying a kite provides the poet as a father with a means of introducing his sons to an exhilarating experience but with a certain note of foreboding

'Flying a kite' has a secondary meaning of trying out an idea, venturing a suggestion to gauge its reception by others. In this poem, although there is an actual, tactile kite, it is also true that the kite is always about to take off and become something else in the series of **similes** and **metaphors**. Written in irregular, **free verse** sections, the poem has no straight narrative line. It shifts from the past to the present tense in line 12 but in the first half there are different pasts: a general description of 'that Sunday afternoon', then a memory of how the kite had been made, and then a curious combination of past and present: 'But now it was'. The opening of the poem is odd:

> All through that Sunday afternoon
> a kite flew above Sunday

Does '*that* Sunday' point to the particular day when the kite was ready to be flown or does it refer to a special Sunday when flying a kite was in some way incongruous? We are not told but the second line gives a special status to the kite, it was 'above Sunday' and all that Sunday meant. The physicality and sense of release are given in line 3 and reiterated through the poem. The details of making the kite seem transcended by the behaviour of the finished object in flight. Shifts of size, from a lark to a heavy shoal of fish in section 3, catch the light lift and the fierce pull of the kite, and Seamus Heaney emphasises these seemingly contradictory qualities in section 4. The aspiration to rise beyond the ordinary bounds, to be like a soaring lark or a soul with no weight, is repeatedly checked by the images of weight and effort, and so, to an extent, we are not unprepared for the 'pull of grief' and the 'strain' of the final section. Although the kite, and perhaps the poem, is 'for' his sons, they are not invited to participate till the final section and then they are not asked to feel the excitement and lift of the kite but, rather, something of our heavy earth straining for release. Nonetheless, the exhilaration of the activity is very definitely there in the poem in a variety of sensations, for example, of tautness ('tightened drumhead') and eccentric fluttering ('blown chaff'). The kite reaches out almost beyond our world but lifts our solid world with its strength, 'like a furrow assumed into the heavens' (line 16). In the end its sustaining wind will slacken and it will tumble back to earth but the enterprise of making and flying it is an invitation into something beyond the earthly.

drumhead tight skin of a drum

chaff husks of corn separated from the grains

grey and slippy painted so that the surface tightens as it dries

bellied hung in a great curve (used to describe a sail) with a suggestion of weight

shoal a large number of fish caught in a net

snipe small wading bird

furrow long strip of earth

assumed received miraculously into Heaven

STATION ISLAND

GENERAL NOTE

Station Island in Lough Derg, County Donegal, has associations with a legendary fast by St Patrick, the patron saint of Ireland, and has been a place of pilgrimage, famous throughout Europe, from medieval times on. The pilgrim, fasting and deprived of sleep, spends three days on the island, walking bare-footed round the circuit or 'station' of prayer-sites or 'beds' praying, confessing and having spiritual fellowship with other penitents. Seamus Heaney himself went on the pilgrimage three times when he was a schoolboy. Various writers before Seamus Heaney have used the subject of the pilgrimage in their work; these include Pedro Calderón, William Carleton, W.B. Yeats, Sean O'Faolain and Patrick

Kavanagh. Seamus Heaney's poem consists of twelve sections, most of which present an encounter between the poet/narrator and a ghost, sometimes a writer, sometimes a person connected biographically with Seamus Heaney. Each encounter poses a challenge to the poet's moral and literary values. The twelve sections display a wide variety of **verse** forms and **dramatic voices**. In the volume called *Station Island*, the sequence poem is Part Two; Part One consists of a collection of individual poems, and Part Three, entitled 'Sweeney Redivivus' (Sweeney Remade), which is a series of poems based on, or in the **persona** of, Mad Sweeney.

    Station Island was published shortly after *Sweeney Astray*, Seamus Heaney's translation of *Buile Suibhne*, a medieval sequence of writings, mainly verse, on the story of Sweeney. Sweeney was a king in seventh-century Ulster who, because he treated the new Christian Church with disrespect, was cursed by Ronan and became an exile but with the gift of flying. He lived wild, half-bird and half-human, mad but with a sensitivity to nature, a broken king with a wonderful command of language. For Seamus Heaney, he was emblematic of a clash of loyalties, a fierce sense of place and a licence to be outrageous and inventive.

SECTION VII   **In this section of the sequence, the poet/narrator is confronted by the ghost of a contemporary of Seamus Heaney, a shopkeeper, who was murdered in a sectarian killing. The ghost relates how he was killed and the poet has to try to come to terms with the horror**

Written in a loose kind of **terza rima**, the section is, in the main, a narrative poem. Unlike strict terza rima, as in Dante's *Divine Comedy*, the **stanzas** here are not linked to each other by **rhyme** but few of the stanzas end with a full stop and the run-on stanzas help to keep the flow of the story moving. The proportions of the poem are rather odd in that the living person, Seamus Heaney, has much less to say than the dead man and, in the end, nothing has been explained and the poet and the reader have to make sense of the story as best they are able. It is when the poet is in vacancy of thought, 'on not being concentrated', that the ghost emerges in his consciousness. The initial shock of recognition and horror contains an element of guilt, 'I was reluctant', developed later on in the plea for forgiveness. After the briefest introduction in lines 12–14, the grocer launches into the story of his murder. There is no obvious attempt at dramatising or commenting on the incident. Even the repetition of 'knocking' and the use of the vulgar 'shites' seem natural to the story. Although we know what happens from the beginning, 'His brow / was blown open above the eye and blood / had dried on his neck and cheek', our suspense, like that of Seamus Heaney, is in the why rather than the what. We too want to ask, 'Did they say nothing?' Why did they choose the grocer? There is no detail in the man's domestic or commercial situation, no mention of political or religious affiliation, which offers any explanation. The man, straightforward and down-to-earth in life, appears not to have or expect to have any greater understanding in death: '"Forgive / my eye," he said, "all that's above my head."' The horrible arbitrariness of the murder makes ideas of punishment ('jail') and forgiveness irrelevant. The grocer is 'the perfect, clean, unthinkable victim', for whose death sectarian revenge or state justice can provide no recompense.

   Throughout the poem there is an odd mixture of factual, ordinary detail and a fearfulness. The wife registers more immediately the frightening possibilities in the knocking in the middle of the night. Without knowing anything, she fears the worst; they are in a society at a time when people have to be prepared for bad news. Her husband knows his murderers 'to see', it is a small community. The callers, however, are prepared to play on the grocer's sympathy – 'There's a child not well' – to entice him to open the door. Later there is a contrast between the 'barefaced' men and the 'open-faced' grocer. 'Barefaced' contains a chilly, ironic ambiguity of 'undisguised' but also 'shameless'. Something unchanged by death in his boyhood friend, and his easy, amiable reminders of playing football together and courting girls, strike the poet/narrator like an accusation or a challenge, as if to say, 'Why are you still alive?' or 'What are you doing about this mess?' He blurts out, 'Forgive the way I have lived indifferent – / forgive my timid circumspect involvement.' Actually, and we must remind ourselves that the pilgrimage in 'Station Island' is a penitential exercise, the accusation is a self-accusation in Seamus Heaney and one to which he has no clear answer. His friend brushes aside the highfalutin stuff about forgiveness but the question remains for the poet after the ghost fades.

barometer instrument for measuring changes in atmospheric pressure
(perhaps, here, the water registers the changes in his moods)
head astray mad
Shop! call for service
sportscoat jacket
pills ... bottle medicine
uniform dress of one of the para-military groups in Northern Ireland
be-all and the end-all the absolute powers, the top people
Austin make of car
rangy tall and long-legged
circumspect cautious, guarded
my eye term of dismissal, of nonsense
stun paralysis

Section xii   This final section of the sequence describes the
narrator returning from the island and receiving
advice on life and art from the ghost of James Joyce.
The original version of the poem has an extra passage
of half a dozen lines (between lines 35 and 36 of the
version in *Selected Poems*)

At various points in 'Station Island', the poet has encountered voices
subversive of the whole penitential enterprise of his pilgrimage. The
final heretical voice is that of one of the most powerful artistic
figures in literature, James Joyce. In Joyce's novel *A Portrait of the
Artist as a Young Man* (1916), the autobiographically based character
Stephen Dedalus says: 'When the soul of a man is born in this country
[Ireland] there are nets flung at it to hold it back from flight. You
talk to me of nationality, language, religion. I shall try to fly by those
nets.' And later he declares: 'I will not serve that in which I no longer
believe, whether it call itself my home, my fatherland or my church: and
I will try to express myself in some mode of life or art as freely as
I can and as wholly as I can, using for my defence the only arms I allow
myself to use – silence, exile and cunning.' The rebellious, individualistic
figure in these declarations is very similar to the ghost of Joyce in
'Station Island' and represents one of the voices or claims in Seamus
Heaney's head.

The section opens as the poet-pilgrim returns from the hallucinatory atmosphere of the island to the everyday, solid world of tarmac and litter baskets. The narrative reaches line 10 before he recognises the man whose hand has helped him onto the jetty. Before Joyce speaks, a memory of his voice comes back to Seamus Heaney. When he speaks, he utters criticisms and imperatives, reiterating that the poet must follow his own individual initiative: 'What you do you must do on your own' and 'You've listened long enough. Now strike your note.' His opening statement seems to demolish any possible worth in the poet's pilgrimage: 'Your obligation / is not discharged by any common rite.' Joyce issues a series of clipped, categorical statements and no opportunity is given for the poet to answer or question 'the harangue and jeers / going on and on'. The very verse form, full terza rima with its interlocking rhyme scheme, drives the poem on, not to a calm resolution of Seamus Heaney's self-doubts, but to a radical challenge of where he is in his life as a man and an artist. As he landed from the holy island, there was an omen of disquiet in the 'alien comfort' he sensed, and Joyce brutally devastates what the middle-aged Seamus Heaney has struggled to achieve, describing it as 'old whinges' which he should have left behind, as 'a cod's game, infantile, like this peasant pilgrimage'. And yet there is something in what Joyce says that is already known by Seamus Heaney, and is both feared and hoped for: 'It was as if I had stepped free into space / alone with nothing that I had not known / already'. Joyce's destructiveness and challenge are drastic but liberating.

The juxtaposing of images of hardness and softness has an effect both bracing and comforting. There is the prosecutor and also the singer, the 'quick and clean' decisiveness and 'dreaming the sun in the sunspot of a breast', the 'harangue' and the 'allurements'. Joyce feels that he had sorted out the mess of nationalism, language and religion but the issues remain contentious half a century later. Of course, the poem, the whole sequence, is a fiction and a device for Seamus Heaney to interrogate and assess himself. The dramatic confrontation with Joyce, however, gives a sharpness to this assessment. The final three sentences in Joyce's voice are in line with Joyce's own attitude but the language of 'probes, allurements' is very much Seamus Heaney. The cloudburst at the end is an emotional release but also, in the image of the 'screens', acts like a curtain coming down to close the theatrical performance.

convalescent recovering from an illness (odd image for someone returning from an attempt to find spiritual health)

seemed blind Joyce's eyesight deteriorated severely as he grew older

rush straight slender stemmed plant growing in boggy ground

ash plant walking stick made from young ash tree (Joyce often carried one)

eddying ... rivers indistinct liquid sound of his voice (reference to Joyce's playing with the names of rivers and water sounds in his novel *Finnegans Wake*. There is a recording of Joyce reading a famous section.)

prosecutor's accusing

singer's Joyce had a wonderful singing voice

narcotic hypnotic

steel nib old fashioned pen

rite ritual, ceremony

sackcloth and the ashes symbols of penitence

English language in Joyce's *A Portrait of the Artist as a Young Man* (1916), Stephen thinks about how English has replaced Irish in Ireland but of how the Irish people and writers have learned to master it

subject people the Irish as colonised by the English

cod's fool's

peasant ignorant, superstitious, backward

redeem gain

decent publicly acceptable

circle wide seemingly tolerant acceptance but actually a kind of net

element surroundings

signatures ... frequency writings in your style, according to your inclination

echo ... allurements different kinds of exploration

elver-gleams shining of young eels (eels move to the sea after they are born and spend time in the ocean)

fumed steamed on the hot surface

IN THE BEECH

This is the fourth poem in a group of twenty in a section entitled 'Sweeney Redivivus'. Seamus Heaney uses the figure of Sweeney (see p. 38), an outcast with the power of flight, but many of the poems in the sequence are 'imagined in contexts far removed from early medieval Ireland' (*Station Island*, p. 123). In this poem, more obviously personal than many of the others, Seamus Heaney looks back to his late teens and a development in his self-awareness

The phrase 'My tree of knowledge' in the second last line reminds the reader that the beech tree has a complex and ambivalent significance. In the Biblical story of Adam and Eve the tree of Knowledge is the forbidden tree and eating its fruit brings sin and death into Eden. The beech tree is a vantage point, a 'listening post', but is also restricted, 'hidebound'; it is 'a strangeness and a comfort'. From it in the poem he looks back into memories of childhood and, as a lookout, anticipates a future. The tree was not special to him because it was part of nature; indeed it could have been made of stone just as well as of wood: 'was it bark or masonry?' It was a secret observation tower from which he could view goings-on around the village: 'I watched' ... 'I felt'. He was on a boundary but he was also the centre, the 'cynosure' of his awareness. There is a striking conjunction of **images** linking the growing boy to the happenings around him. Initially we have the bullocks churning up the smelly mud almost as a suitable setting for the boy's secretive exploration of his sexual sensations, and this sexual consciousness is perhaps continued in the way he sees the tree and the chimney in the third and fourth sections as a mixture of natural and non-natural elements, of growth and rigidity. Even the militaristic images of the tanks and aeroplane, probably recalled from his childhood during the Second World War when American forces trained nearby, have an excitement and vigour which look back to the young bulls of line 3. Of course, the instruments of imperial power also look forward to the 1980s and the occupation forces of the British army. Like a boy given a task and then forgotten, the Heaney/Sweeney of the poem is still a lookout and his poetry is a kind of listening post,

STATION ISLAND: IN THE BEECH continued

'thick-tapped, soft-fledged'. The words 'book' and 'beech' probably share a root.

concrete suggests newness, perhaps constructed by the army

bullocks young bulls (usually desexed)

covert shelter under the trees

reek powerful smell (of animals and mud)

column smooth stone pillar (the bark of the beech is smooth and close-fitting to the trunk)

bole trunk of tree

puzzled grew tentatively as if searching

milk-tooth ... tapers new, soft, irregular shaped leaves

chimney of a new factory or mill

stamen male reproductive organ of a flower

course by course stage by stage

antics work (but the height and scale make the men seem unimportant or silly)

cynosure centre of attention (the heart of the trunk of the tree)

imperium absolute power

refreshed reiterated

bolt-mark rivets on the metal tracks of the tanks

hidebound restricted in its viewpoint (and the bark is like a tight skin)

thick-tapped solid, deeply rooted

soft-fledged with young foliage like new feathers on a bird almost ready for flight

THE FIRST FLIGHT

See Poem 2 of Extended Commentaries

FROM THE HAW LANTERN (1987)

FROM THE FRONTIER OF WRITING

The poem is concerned with the sense of being interrogated, first at a military check-point and, second, as a writer facing public appraisal of the work

This is one of four poems in the collection *The Haw Lantern* with similar titles. The other three are 'From the Republic of Conscience', 'From the

Land of the Unspoken' and 'From the Canton of Expectation'. They read like reports from a symbolic rather than a geographical location and each of them operates as a parable with a mixture of physical and abstract elements. In 'From the Frontier of Writing' the use of 'you' generalises the experience and the reader feels included in the situation. The poem, written in rough terza rima stanzas, divides into two equal halves but the imagery of intimidating military scrutiny is common to both. The four stanzas of the first half are all one long, involved sentence holding in the 'you' and the reader. The opening lines are not quite grammatical but have an immediacy of atmosphere, of helplessness and paralysis, wonderfully caught in the word 'nilness' invented by Seamus Heaney. Nothing is said, there is no sound, and the release in line 8 has no human softening. The driver does nothing dramatic; rather he affects an unconcern. The fear is palpable and the intimidation has had its effect as the driver moves off 'subjugated, yes, and obedient', a confession of weakness. 'So' in line 13 is an oddly casual connective between the two halves. The frontier of writing occurs when the writer tries to achieve something in writing and submits himself or herself to public appraisal. For Seamus Heaney to present the border crossing and the frontier of writing in the same terms has a comical side to it and Seamus Heaney may be mocking the fuss of a public performance with cameramen ('guns on tripods'), the chairman introducing the poet (the 'data'), and the lighting technician 'out of the sun'. Or the frontier may be the scrutiny of reviewers and critics. Nonetheless, and allowing for a satirical reading, the poem has a graver tone and a stronger note of relief. 'Arraigned yet freed' is a large phrase; he has been called to account, accused, censured, made to feel guilty or inadequate, before he is released and can put the trial behind him. The poem concludes with the images from the earlier border crossing and we share the liberation from the interrogating figures now 'flowing and receding' behind the car. The primary focus of the poem is not on the first border and the military roadblock but on the frontier on which the writer operates and where he or she is judged; he uses the imagery of the first to describe the second. It may be that if Seamus Heaney's chilling experience of border crossing is based particularly on his journeys from the Republic back to Northern Ireland, his frontier of writing ('So you drive on') is particularly in his home territory where his every public gesture is scrutinised and interpreted.

subjugated rendered powerless, made submissive

squawk / of clearance signal on his radio that the driver may proceed

current stream carrying him forward

CLEARANCES

GENERAL NOTE

'Clearances' consists of eight **sonnets** with different rhyme schemes, written as **elegies** for Seamus Heaney's mother who died in 1984. By the title 'Clearances' he may be suggesting several ideas. Tidying up and removing debris is a clearance. People removed forcibly from the land in Scotland and Ireland in the nineteenth century were 'cleared'. 'Clearance' is the permission given for a ship or aeroplane to land or take off. 'Clearance' is the approved distance between moving ships. A clearance is the space left empty when something has been removed.

SONNET III **Sonnet III recalls sharing the task of peeling potatoes with his mother when he was a boy and how that memory came back to him when his mother was dying**

In the **octave** the **rhymes** are very imperfect perhaps matching the incompleteness of the relationship between the son and his mother. They share a task and the silence is amicable but there is something lacking, hinted at in the phrase 'Cold comforts'. The word 'weeping' in the previous line, although a wonderfully accurate word for solder dripping off the iron, introduces a suggestion of unhappiness. Absent from Mass, they, nonetheless, enjoy a communion in the domestic ritual of peeling the potatoes and slipping them into the bucket of clean water. The second part of the **sonnet** comes into the present at the death bed of his mother. He cannot join in the prayers, disparagingly describing the priest's gusto as 'hammer and tongs', but comes close to his dying mother by recalling that earlier communion when they were so much in harmony. In the final line there is a touch of regret that the early rapport was not developed. Affection for his mother is clear but there was also a gap between them. Perhaps it would have been better if other tasks and responsibilities had not so often brought them 'to [their] senses' (line 8) and out of their togetherness, a togetherness pointed to in the simplest of vocabularies.

solder soft metal alloy melted and used to join or repair metal parts
Cold comforts literally the peeled potatoes in the water; but the phrase is used to mean poor consolations
hammer and tongs with energy and noise, **ironically** used
responding joining in the prayers
fluent deft, with easy movements

SONNET V   **Seamus Heaney recalls folding bed sheets with his mother which have been freshly washed and dried on the clothes line outside**

The **sonnet** is in two equal sentences and is a demonstration of Seamus Heaney's ability to describe a procedure economically and accurately in the confines of a **verse** form. The **rhymes** are unobtrusive, partly because they are mainly **half-rhymes** and partly because so many of the lines are not end-stopped, but the pattern of regular line length and the criss-cross of rhymes enact the pulling and folding of the sheets between the two people. The movements involved in dealing with the sheets are like a dance where the partners pull away from each other and come together, where strength is used but always in accordance with the two people and the requirements of the task. In the second sentence when the mother and son briefly touch hands on the final folding of a sheet, we are made aware of an awkwardness, certainly on the boy's part. Line 10 is itself awkward to read and seems to trip over itself in the **syntax** and repeated words. There is even a mild pun in 'Beforehand' or 'before hand' and the **image** of the game of noughts and crosses fits playfully with the diagonal and vertical pullings on the sheets but also conveys a mild competitiveness and incompatibility. Mother and son share comfortably in the simple domestic chore, almost a ritual in the practised, fixed movements, and in the financial situation where the family sheets have been made out of squares of old flour sacks, but a gap or a restraint is there also: 'Coming close again by holding back'. They are 'hand to hand' not hand in hand, and 'for a split second as if nothing had happened'. What constitutes the gap between them is not specified; could it be the generational difference or gender or temperament? Notwithstanding the gap, the affection in the poem is strong.

FROM THE HAW LANTERN: CLEARANCES: SONNET V continued

undulating curving like a wave

thwack sound of the flapped sheet, slower and fuller than 'crack'

touch and go brief encounter but the phrase also means uncertain

x … o game played on a sheet of paper divided into nine squares where the object is for the person who is X to make a line of three Xs and prevent the other person making a line of Os, each marking a square in turn

flour sacks linen bags used to carry a hundredweight (about 50 kilos) of flour

FROM SEEING THINGS (1991)

THE SETTLE BED

The subject of the poem is an unwieldy piece of furniture but the poem is concerned with how we handle our inheritance

Matching the settle bed, the poem has a ponderous quality. The long-lined **triplets** have none of the impetus of the **terza rima** of which Seamus Heaney is often fond. It is impossible to read it quickly; apart from the final **stanza**, there is no flow. Heavily adjectival, the poem is cluttered and the movement is impeded. The opening three lines are each a sentence without an active verb and the hyphenated words prevent any momentum. Made almost as part of a traditional rural house, in a modern house this mongrel piece of furniture is cumbersome, hardly functional and always in the way. It is emblematic of a way of life now passed, the time of his parents and grandparents. It may be that he occasionally slept in such a bed when he was a child. He presents it now largely in terms of other articles of the past: 'Trunk', 'cart', 'pew', 'bin', 'ark', 'funeral ship' and the bedtime routines of the old rural Ulster. In line 13 he attempts to come back into the present: 'And now this is an "inheritance"' but the dash marks a return to the unmanageable qualities of the object. In line 18 he tries again to find a way of coping with the 'un-get-roundable weight' of the object and he finds a way through a whimsical fantasy of hundreds of settle beds falling on the people. The wildness of this vision allows him to declare that 'whatever is given / Can always be reimagined' and prepares the way for the final joke or surreal image of the lookout who saw so far ahead, such a different world, that the actual world had altered by the time he descended the mast. What Seamus Heaney is affirming is the power of human vision or poetic imagination to transform the given, the inheritance, however obtuse, awkward or unsuitable that given may seem.

In the context of Northern Ireland an extraordinary vision is needed, not to deny the difficult legacy of the past, but to make something new from it and see beyond it. The settle bed was a sofa, a bed and a chest but not very wonderful as any of them and Northern Ireland itself is a curious mixture of differences but not a fortunate amalgamation of them. The dense language of the poem does not underestimate the obduracy and ignorance of the inheritance but it also treasures the solidities, reliability and contentments in that tradition. In the end, Seamus Heaney's poem offers an optimistic view that people can learn 'to conquer that weight', the burden of the past in the present, although an optimism resting on such a tall story may also contain a doubt.

Settle Bed wooden bench with storage chest, can be adapted for use as a box bed

Willed down left in a will to be given to a named relative

Trunk-hasped with metal fastenings as you would find on a travelling trunk

ignorant unsophisticated, basic

pew-strait narrow and severe as the enclosed benches in a church

ark wooden chest (or the crude boat made by Noah)

cribbed confined

seasoned deal dried and aged planks of pine, commonly used in coffins

unkindled unlit

funeral ship Viking chiefs when they died were launched on to the sea in ornate funeral ships which were set on fire

measure as for a coffin

headboard wooden head-end of the bed

Unpathetic uttered by habit rather than in deep feeling

och ... hohs groans of weariness

Anthems characteristic sounds

the Bible, the beads centre of Protestant and Catholic prayers respectively

ridge-tiles of the roof

Again and again and again emphasising the persistence of the tradition

cargoed loaded with

THE SETTLE BED continued

tongue-and-groove way in which planks fit together tightly
dower gift of nature, endowment
barrage bombardment
Plank-thick a phrase for 'stupid' is 'thick as two planks'
hull-stupid stupid as a wall
joker teller of tall stories
posted high commanded to climb to the top of the ship's mast to try to see beyond the fog

GLANMORE REVISITED

THE SKYLIGHT – VII

> Glanmore is in the Wicklow Hills south of Dublin where Seamus Heaney has a cottage. This sequence of seven sonnets echoes the ten 'Glanmore Sonnets' published in *Field Work* (1979). This sonnet concerns a disagreement he has with his wife as to whether or not a window should be introduced in the roof of the cottage attic

The opening sentence has a conversational feel. Although the 'You' wins the argument in the poem, she does not reappear. The space between the octave and the sestet of the sonnet form marks the change from the speaker's old way of thinking to his new one. In fact, however, the pleasure taken in the poem by the reader is not in winning an argument or in a superior sensation in the sestet; rather, both ways of seeing the attic are pleasurable. Seamus Heaney conveys his enjoyment in the closed-in security of the sealed attic and also the lit-up release when the window is cut in the roof. The title describes not simply the window but the whole exposure to the light of the sky. In the octave the rhymes are very obvious, keeping things as they were, sealing in the cosy enclosure. All the descriptive phrases emphasise the shut-in snugness under the roof, the 'trunk-lid fit of the old ceiling', 'all hutch and hatch'.

In the sestet the rhymes are looser, reflecting the sense of liberation, and everything is 'extravagant' and 'wide open'. The biblical story of the man cured by Jesus has the appropriate largeness; in a sense, the roof has to be broken before he can be healed and walk freely. Looking back, we see that there was something too protective, too inward about the closed attic; now the poet has the confidence to face outward. For him, like the man with the palsy, there is a kind of salvation, 'his sins forgiven'.

seasoned aged

tongue-and-groove tight-fitting joint holding planks together

pitch pine pine wood rich in resin and commonly used in wooden ceilings

claustrophobic shut-in

snuff-dry as dry as powdered tobacco

hutch a small box or house as for a rabbit

hatch heavy lid

that house where Jesus was when the man came hoping to be healed. The crowd around Jesus was so great that the man on his bed was lowered through the roof (Luke 5)

palsy a paralysis with involuntary shaking

LIGHTENINGS – VIII

> Part II of the collection *Seeing Things* is called 'Squarings' and consists of four groups of twelve poems each with twelve lines arranged in unrhyming triplets. The first group is called 'Lightenings'. Number VIII recounts a legendary story of a miraculous air ship which appeared to the monks at Clonmacnoise

The poem appears to be a straight retelling of an incident found in the annals of the monastery; the 'poetry' is in the incident itself and, Seamus Heaney seems to suggest, needs no ornament or elaboration. We assume that the oratory is open to the sky but the ship is in the air not on the sea. The centre of the story is in the recognition by the abbot that the human, earthly atmosphere is foreign and fatal to the man from the ship as land and air might be to a mermaid. When the anchor is disentangled from the altar-rail and the ship moves off, the sailor no doubt tells his companions of the strange creatures he met below. The poem asks a question about what is normal and what is miraculous. Can they be interchangeable? The monks themselves inhabit a curious dimension, being in the world but also out of it. In prayer they detach themselves from the ordinary world and as Christians they accept the miraculous as part of God's nature. Certainly they seem to see something extraordinary in their oratory but, to the visitor, they appear miraculous. Seamus

Heaney quietly disturbs our complacent distinction between the ordinary and the miraculous.

annals records of events recorded in monasteries. The Annals of Clonmacnoise contain details from the earliest times down to the fifteenth century

Clonmacnoise monastery established in the centre of Ireland probably in the sixth century. It enjoyed great renown as a centre of scholarship and holiness

oratory place of prayer, often a small chapel

shinned climbed using feet and hands

abbot head of the monastery

FROM THE SPIRIT LEVEL (1996)

A SOFA IN THE FORTIES

Childhood make-believe is the subject although a wider context of world events in the 1940s is indicated

The poem consists of four equal parts each written in four **stanzas** of unrhymed **terza rima**. The ordering of the parts is odd and significant. We might expect that Seamus Heaney would begin by describing the sofa (part 2), move to the children's game with it, and conclude with the reference to the wider world. However, he obviously wishes to begin and end the poem with the make-believe world of the children. The sofa is situated in the kitchen, the centre of activity in the Heaney farmhouse, but adults are barely mentioned; this is a children's realm. In parts 1 and 4 the fantasy train is wonderfully evoked with all the appropriate movements and noises and the children's absorption is total. The phrase 'with all our might' has a childlike intensity. There is no scepticism in the minds of the children: 'Constancy was its own reward already'. Even off-duty as the sofa is in part 2, it still has its special air, its potential to be more than it is at present, to become 'heavenbound'. This is a world of utter possibility where 'speed and distance were inestimable', and 'transported' in the final line carries the added sense of being enchanted into a new dimension of pleasure. The sofa in itself with its 'Black leatherette and ornate gauntness' has nothing to commend it, not even comfort; but in the imaginative minds of the children it can never be ordinary. 'Flotation' and 'pageantry' indicate this special quality. In the midst of this fantasy phase where, even with 'insufficient toys', they live with a heightened grasp of possibility, another world makes claims on them, a world of 'history and ignorance'. The radio introduces the children to an alien culture which has all the authority of the BBC and the British establishment. What the BBC reports on is 'history' and the children are made aware of their ignorance of this history. The phrase 'Between him and us / A great gulf was fixed' echoes a verse in the Bible (Luke 16:26) which describes the total difference between Heaven and Hell. The allusion, if it is such, seems extravagant but certainly Seamus Heaney is contrasting strongly the child's imaginative and flexible world and the 'absolute' world of the radio 'where pronunciation/Reigned tyrannically'. The power of that language and all it represents and promotes is seductive and destructive in the simple but rich minds of the Heaney children. In the final lines of the poem there is an initiation suggested in the **image** of the children pouring through a tunnel but perhaps there is also, in the image of the 'unlit carriages through fields at night', a veiled reference to the wagons carrying victims towards extermination camps under the Nazis in the domain of 'history and ignorance', a reference anticipated in the earlier 'Ghost-train? Death-gondola?'

> **forties** 1940s when Seamus Heaney was a child
>
> **pistons** mechanism which conveys power to the wheels in a steam engine (the movement of the elbows imitates the action of the pistons)
>
> **jamb-wall** outside wall of the kitchen
>
> **shunted** moved the train from one set of rails to another
>
> **invisible** imaginary tickets
>
> **Went giddy** wobbled
>
> **unreachable ones** imaginary people waiting to greet them on their arrival
>
> **Ghost-train** train in a funfair where there are frightening, ghostly happenings
>
> **Death-gondola** in Venice there are special funeral gondolas, the ornate boats peculiar to the city
>
> **leatherette** imitation leather
>
> **castors** small wheels
>
> **fluent** lavishly curved
>
> **superannuated pageantry** old-fashioned stylishness

heavenbound elevated beyond the ordinary
earthbound solid and reliable
add ... down things more unpredictable
wireless radio
'The Riders of the Range' radio serial set in the Wild West
Fit for prepared to suffer
craned leaned over
run the gauntlet endured all dangers and difficulties

ST KEVIN AND THE BLACKBIRD

The poem tells the story of St Kevin and the blackbird
which nests in his hand. It asks questions about the nature
of Kevin's act

The two halves of the poem are of equal length and are written in
the same verse form of unrhymed triplets. The first part is descriptive
and relates what took place; the second is speculative and tries to
imagine what the saint felt and thought. The poem opens casually as if
the speaker is listing a series of examples; but examples of what? The
second part has a similar casual, even dismissive, feel in the phrase 'the
whole thing' and 'anyhow'. Is the story a fiction ('imagined') without
any basis in actual events? The poem is not attempting to establish
the authenticity of the happening although the incident is described
straightforwardly as it might have taken place. Rather, Seamus Heaney is
inviting the reader to imagine himself or herself into this extraordinary
situation attributed to Kevin. What would such an experience feel
like? Could Kevin's monastic Christian training have enabled him to
endure such a situation? Could he detach his mind from the discomfort
of his body? The ending of the poem is ambivalent. The poet/narrator
offers a striking image of the immobile saint as having gone beyond
the need for reward or even release, the 'labour' is sufficient in itself. He
has become his prayer. However, to achieve such a detachment is to be
empty of all feeling for self or bird or river; he is in such a suspended
animation that it is a kind of death, a 'shut-eyed blank', and is beyond
the pity of line 10. The delicacy of the bird with its 'tucked / Neat head
and claws' has no meaning for him, there is no longer a sense of 'the
network of eternal life'. There is a suggestion of something comical in

Kevin's position in the first half which disappears in the enigmatic conclusion.

> **Kevin** Irish saint (died 618) founded a monastery at Glendalough. Many legends portray his love for nature
>
> **cell** individual's room in monastery
>
> **crossbeam** structural beam of wood across the width of a building
>
> **eternal** everlasting or, perhaps, in the sense of on-going
>
> **fledged** equipped with feathers
>
> **shut-eyed blank of underearth** emptiness of a buried dead body
>
> **love's deep river** total dedicated love of a Christian saint

'POET'S CHAIR' Prompted by contemplating a piece of urban sculpture in the shape of a chair, Seamus Heaney has some thoughts on artifice and nature, time and eternity

The scope of reference in this poem is very wide, including, for example, Leonardo da Vinci, Yeats, Socrates, Apollo, as well as the sculptor, random passers-by in Dublin, the poet's father and himself, and it swings about between contemporary Dublin and Athens, cities and the countryside. The sculptured chair in Dublin changes to the chair in Athens in which the condemned Socrates spent his final hours and then to the poet's sitting place in a field when he was younger. People are out on the town, Socrates, the philosopher, is dying, Mr Heaney is ploughing a field. The focus keeps shifting. Apart from remarking in the opening line of part 2 that he is the observer, the poet does not emerge in his own person till the third part. The three unrhymed parts of the poem are prefaced with a rhyming quatrain. Leonardo's theory of painting relies heavily on the relations of light and shade. The sun, from its point of view, is always full-on to an object and, therefore, cannot see shadows. The sculptor, able to walk round the object being sculpted, has to be aware of angles seen from different positions and the interplay of solid to shadow as the perspective changes. The image of the sculptor as a lover, tied in a connection of changeability and fixity, introduces the emotional force of the sculpted chair. With its animal feet and leafy branching back, the bronze chair, set in a city courtyard, is a mixture of inanimate object, living creatures and growing nature, the city and the country. It is because of this mixture that passers-by take such pleasure in sitting on it and they feel that they become part of the mixture and enlarge their sense of themselves; in this way the chair is a place of imagination, hence a 'poet's chair'. An elevation of spirit is announced in the sentence beginning, 'Once out of nature', an allusion to Yeats's poem 'Sailing to Byzantium' where there is a conflict between artifice and changeable nature. In a way typical of Seamus Heaney, the high-flown notion is immediately undercut and even mocked with the dismissive phrase, 'Or something like that', followed by the philistine cynicism of a passer-by, *'Leaves / On a bloody chair! Would you believe it?'* The chair is, among other things, a piece of fun, a cause of amusement and a piece of street furniture.

Seamus Heaney's mind, thinking about the chair, is cast back to the last days of Socrates who, condemned to death, insisted on sitting with his friends, calmly discussing philosophical issues. Because the boat had to return from Delos before his execution could take place, his life was extended by thirty days while the arrival of the boat was awaited. The philosopher had convinced himself of the immortality of the soul and was remarkably cheerful. In the poem these final days of Socrates are represented as luminous and optimistic about the life after death. Somehow he has, in his chair in the prison, managed to imagine a world of permanency, and for him the imagined is the real world. The poem in the third part moves to the vantage point enjoyed by the poet when he was younger sitting against the thorn tree at the centre of his father's field. As in the previous two parts there is an act of imagining, of 'foreknowledge', in the poet's state of heightened awareness: 'The horses are all hoof / And burnished flank'. It is as if the younger Seamus Heaney can see ahead to when his poetry can do its kind of digging across time (as he has demonstrated earlier in the poem), when his present seat will become the poet's chair, and when he will believe in his notion of permanence: 'Of being here for good'. The poem ends on a large, benedictory note: 'Of being here for good in every sense'.

> **'Poet's Chair'** piece of sculpture by Carolyn Mulholland, a contemporary artist from Northern Ireland and a friend of the poet
>
> **Leonardo** Leonardo da Vinci (1452–1519), Renaissance Italian painter and inventor. He filled many notebooks with comments on art
>
> *qui vive* alert, on duty

splay-foot broad, out-turned foot

flibbertigibbet aimless or frivolous person

Old birds eccentric old women

boozers drunk people

pissers stray men or urinating men

winged the branches are like wings

graft the branches growing out of the seat

Socrates Greek philosopher (469–399BC), condemned to death by Athenian court for allegedly introducing strange gods and corrupting the youth of the city. His final days are described in his disciple Plato's work *Phaedo*

bald as a coot mildly mocking description of Socrates's bald head

verdant green with vegetation

Apollo's shrine on the island of Delos a holy place was instituted by the ancient Greeks to honour Apollo and the Athenians each year commemorated the liberation of their city by performing ceremonies on the island and bringing a ship back to Athens covered in plants. No public events could happen in Athens till the ship returned to the city

hemlock the poison Socrates was given with which to end his life

Crito close friend of Socrates

ache / Deferred the execution is delayed for thirty days

lea fallow, unploughed in the previous year

thorn tree type of thorny tree superstitiously preserved in Ireland. It is considered unlucky to cut them down

burnished smooth and shining

ploughshare blade of the plough

POSTSCRIPT

See Poem 3 of Extended Commentaries

PART THREE

CRITICAL APPROACHES

THEMES

FIDELITY TO PLACES AND PEOPLE OF HIS UPBRINGING

Although Seamus Heaney has travelled all over the world and spent
considerable periods in a variety of places, the centre of gravity in his
poetry has remained very constant. There is a fidelity to the locations,
persons and communal feel of the place where he grew up in Northern
Ireland. In *The Spirit Level* (1996), he has a poem, 'Keeping Going',
dedicated to his brother who remained to farm where they were brought
up in the midst of all the political troubles. He says, with obvious
approval: 'My dear brother, you have good stamina. / You stay on where
it happens'. As so often in his poetry, there is a hint of self-rebuke as if
he has not maintained their inheritance with the commitment shown by
his brother. Nonetheless, as a poet he has, in a very real sense, stayed on
and made his place known. Even simple actions, such as drinking water
in an old woman's house, are recalled with a sense of religious duty:
'Where I have dipped to drink again, to be / Faithful to the
admonishment on her cup, / *Remember the Giver*' ('A Drink of Water' in
Field Work – 1979). And in the preceding poem, 'The Toome Road', the
essence of that childhood community defies the turmoil of the past few
years and 'stands here still ... The invisible, untoppled omphalos' (see
Commentaries).

In Irish Gaelic there is a long tradition of poems called
Dinnshenchas, poems concerned with naming localities and the love
attached to them. Each place holds its own peculiar history, and Seamus
Heaney, from his earliest work and 'Toner's bog' in 'Digging', has
explored and shown off the places of his homeland. There are poems
explicitly about individual places such as 'Anahorish', 'Broagh', 'The
Strand at Lough Beg' and 'At Bannagher' but there are also many such as
'Funeral Rites', 'North', 'The Singer's House' and 'A Retrospect' where an
intimacy with local places plays a significant role in the poetry. Even the
translated poems of *Sweeney Astray* (1982) can be seen as satisfying this

side of the poet. From *The Haw Lantern* (1987) on, the hold of home places has slackened as if he has come to accept that illumination or a sense of belonging is not dependent on childhood memories. Nonetheless, he continues to show that he learned a lesson from these localities, that any place made special by familiarity can be archaeologically dug to reveal its layers or strata of experience: 'I knew the ore of longing in those words' ('Squarings' XLI).

Similarly, he felt obliged in his early writing to record something of the lives of 'his' people and, in particular, the skills and routines of older individuals whose way of living and working was dying out. He was, as he says in a poem called 'Ancestral Photograph' (*Death of a Naturalist*), 'Closing this chapter of our chronicle'. The old processes of a farm, thatching, divining for water, working with horses, eel-fishing, the work of the blacksmith, the oral tradition in music – all are kept alive in Seamus Heaney's poetry. He seems motivated to describe these activities in detail not with nostalgia or regret but rather in admiration of the craftsmanship of baking or digging or whatever. As in his fascination with places where the name has a metaphoric definition akin to a major element in poetry, in the trained feel for materials, the economical movements and expertise of the craftsman he sees a parallel with the writing of poems: 'As you find a rhythm / Working you' ('Casualty').

A central strand in his heritage is obviously his own family. His mother and father and relatives appear throughout the poems. Their activities, aspirations, disappointments, relationships and even deaths anchor the invention of the poetry in something reliable and apparently authentic. His father is introduced with his 'straining rump' ('Digging') and 'broad shadow' ('Follower'), develops with the delicately made harvest bow and shadow rabbit in 'Alphabets', and emerges in the later poems such as 'Man and Boy', 'Seeing Things' and 'The Ash Plant', and the tenderness of remembrance in 'A Call', 'The Errand', 'The Sharping Stone' and 'The Strand'. His mother seldom features in the early poems although, perhaps, 'The Wife's Tale' includes parts of her, and later 'Old Smoothing Iron' is based on memories of her. Her death in 1984 prompted the eight sonnets of 'Clearances'. The relationship of mother and son is presented affectionately but with an acknowledgement of a restraint between them which 'kept them allied and at bay' (IV). Her importance to him is obvious in her absence, 'a space / Utterly empty, utterly a source' (VIII); she taught him how to balance force and gentleness (see Commentaries). The later poem 'Two Lorries' connects a memory of his mother as a young woman and a bomb exploding in neighbouring Magherafelt. 'Mossbawn: Two Poems in Dedication' were written for his aunt Mary; one celebrates the indoor domestic work of making scones; the second describes the annual preparation of seed potatoes for planting and asks the 'calendar customs' to 'compose the frieze / With all of us there'. There is a poem, 'Mid-Term Break', about the death of a young brother killed in a car crash and a pair of poems about the killing of a cousin: 'The Strand at Lough Beg' and the second half of section VIII of 'Station Island'. The clan, the communal group, matters to Seamus Heaney and needs to be named in his song and invoked as a source of strength: 'What do we say any more / to conjure the salt of our earth?' ('The Singer's House').

CHILDHOOD

Childhood features in three different ways in Seamus Heaney's work. There are poems which recall his own growing-up; poems which are concerned with his children's childhood; and poems which use a childlike way of responding to situations.

Many of the poems in his first collection, *Death of a Naturalist* (1966), published when he was twenty-seven, describe incidents from his early years and give an immediate sense of the hopes and fears, the pleasures and pains of childhood experience and his growth towards adulthood. In these poems there is a closeness of focus and all the senses are alert. The language is not childlike but the perspective is. Objects and creatures are presented out of adult proportion: 'The two-lugged sacks moved in like great blind rats' ('The Barn') and there is an intimate connection between physical and emotional experience. An anxiousness or apprehension is often apparent and he clearly identifies with Wordsworth in *The Prelude* and quotes lines from it as an epigraph to 'Singing School':

> *Fair seed-time had my soul, and I grew up*
> *Fostered alike by beauty and by fear;*

As in Wordsworth's poetry, the boy exploring the world of nature often sees himself as an intruder, against whom nature may seek revenge. 'Death of a Naturalist' is an obvious early example but the sense of trespass remains in later poems of remembered childhood such as 'The King of the Ditchbacks'. The pleasures and illumination of childhood reappear throughout the work from 'Follower' when his father, ploughing, 'rode me on his back / Dipping and rising to his plod' to 'A Sofa in the Forties': 'Potentially heavenbound'. In the poem 'Mint', in *The Spirit Level* (1996), recalling the 'heady' smell of the mint cut on Sundays when he was a child, he concludes: 'My last things will be first things slipping from me'.

Being a father allowed Seamus Heaney to experience some childhood situations at second hand. The hazel-wood stick he makes for his daughter to 'play with and pose with' and the kite he makes for his sons reintroduce him to a series of sensations. He takes pleasure when his daughter 'Woke in the dawn and answered doodle doo / To the rooster' ('The Cot' – in *Seeing Things*) and in anticipating his niece growing up in Gloucestershire ('A Peacock's Feather' – in *The Haw Lantern*).

The daring and discoveries of childhood have formed the basis for many poems and provided **imagery** for Seamus Heaney's urge to go beyond the known to touch something new. The collection *Seeing Things* (1991) has a particular density of such poems. In 'Wheels within Wheels' he moves from the pleasure of 'pedalling / (By hand) a bike turned upside down' to 'an access of free power'. The physical is a starting point always leading beyond itself: 'But enough was not enough. Who ever saw / The limit in the given anyhow?' Games of marbles, sliding on ice and football are relived in the poetry, always with relish and a surge of enhancement: 'Was it you / or the ball that kept going / beyond you?' ('Three Drawings' in *Seeing Things*). The child's mind is sometimes less bound by the constraints of physical laws and Seamus Heaney, in recalling childhood's exploits such as swinging, holds on to this imaginative release:

> In spite of all, we sailed
> Beyond ourselves and over and above
> The rafters aching in our shoulderblades,
> The give and take of branches in our arms. ('The Swing')

As his career has progressed the childlike has been accepted with more openness, less worry. This acceptance can be traced by comparing 'Blackberry-Picking', 'Bye-Child', 'The Railway Children', 'Hailstones' and 'Fosterling'.

CELEBRATION

Seamus Heaney's world, whatever its adversities, has always offered a rich store of pleasure from which he could draw:

> And here is love
> like a tinsmith's scoop
> sunk past its gleam
> in the meal-bin. ('Sunlight')

From his childhood on, there is a marked lack of bitterness or grudge and often he emerges as 'one of the venerators' ('Sandstone Keepsake'). Objects, the processes of the natural world, love, people, the crafts of making, and language itself have all elicited an appreciative response. He confesses: 'Me waiting until I was nearly fifty / To credit marvels' ('Fosterling') but his poetry has always celebrated a delight in the world, 'things founded clean on their own shapes' ('The Peninsula').

Certainly there have been concentrations of poems written with special relish. The 'Glanmore Sonnets' are particularly happy as if his move to Wicklow was a blessing: 'It was marvellous / And actual, I said out loud, "A haven"' (Sonnet VII) and there is a special sense of married love. In *Seeing Things* there are many poems of radiant acceptance: 'Time to be dazzled and the heart to lighten' ('Fosterling'). In his earlier work, in the midst of enjoyment, there was often a note of disquiet: '[I] was angry that my trust could not repose / In the clear light' ('Oysters') but in the later poems pleasure is savoured more uncomplicatedly and he can even state: 'I trust contrariness' ('Casting and Gathering' in *Seeing Things*). Simple objects can be emblematic. A pitchfork, familiar to him from childhood, is described in acutely accurate tactile detail but is also, for him, a 'probe' towards where 'perfection – or nearness to it – is imagined' ('The Pitchfork'). Seamus Heaney presents himself as an unexpected guest at a feast: 'I stood in the door, unseen and blazed upon' ('Settings' XV) and his gusto for sensuous sensation is vividly apparent in a rich language. And, although there is no religious or theological interpretation to his reading of the world, there is a spiritual reaching through the sensuous, past the sensuous, to a larger understanding: 'Beyond the range you thought you'd settled for' ('Squarings' XXXIX). The final poem 'Postscript' in *The Spirit Level* catches this mingling of the physical and the spiritual.

HISTORY

Although it would be misleading to describe Seamus Heaney as a heavily historical writer, aspects of the past do feature strongly in his poetry. For the most part, the past is either an Irish past or a past which can be related to Ireland. He is fascinated by historical strata, by how one phase of society derives from or builds on an earlier phase, and how, so often, human culture seems to repeat itself. In 'Bogland' he describes how archaeologists dig down into the bog: 'Every layer they strip / Seems camped on before'; in 'Gifts of Rain' he presents his interest more personally: 'in the shared calling of blood / arrives my need / for antediluvian lore'.

Poems as different and written so far apart as 'Bog Oak' and 'The Thimble' share a sense of continuity and contrast in diverse historical periods. The latter poem juxtaposes the sacred and the profane, the legendary and the ordinary, the ancient and the contemporary. Seamus Heaney's so-called 'Bog' poems, where he uses past incidents to comment on contemporary events, will be discussed in the next section (Morality and Politics).

Ordinary historical happenings and personages do occur occasionally, mainly at pivotal moments in Ireland's story. The period roughly between the fifth and tenth centuries, when Celtic monastic Christianity replaced nature worship and Druidism, has inspired a number of poems including the translation *Sweeney Astray* (1982). Sweeney, it seems, was a king in seventh century Ireland who held to the old order, went mad and was cursed by St Ronan; gifted with the power of flight, this half-historical, half-legendary figure wandered round Ireland and western Scotland composing poems in his embittered madness. This poetic exile with divided loyalties appealed to Seamus Heaney and he used the Sweeney perspective in a series of poems to reflect on various issues. His essay, 'The God in the Tree: Early Irish Nature Poetry' (1978), collected in *Preoccupations* enlarges on his fondness for aspects of this remote culture and he returns to it several times in his later work in poems such as 'Squarings' VIII and 'St Kevin and the Blackbird'.

Viking raids and settlements in the eighth and ninth centuries seriously disrupted the monastic communities and introduced new elements to Irish society. For Seamus Heaney, the Vikings have become an aspect of Irishness, something violent and vigorous, an antithesis to monastic calm, but with their own fierce rituals. The poem 'Viking Dublin: Trial Pieces' explores the Viking legacy. A similar but much more thorough and concerted violence is seen in the Norman, then English, then British occupation of Ireland in the following centuries. Seamus Heaney uses a brutal **imagery** of sexual rape in the poem 'Ocean's Love to Ireland' (*North*) and 'Act of Union': 'The ground possessed and repossessed' … 'the big pain / That leaves you raw, like opened ground, again'. The plantations of the seventeenth century are presented in a general way, without local reference or bitterness. Similarly, the few poems which centre on later events are vivid and painful but they are not part of a systematic reading of Irish history from any markedly partisan position. Examples of such poems are 'Linen Town' (*Wintering Out*), 'Requiem for the Croppies' and 'Wolfe Tone', dealing with the situation at the end of the eighteenth century, and 'At a Potato Digging' and 'For the Commander of the "Eliza"' (*Death of a Naturalist*) which deal with the Famine of the 1840s.

MORALITY AND POLITICS

Seamus Heaney's poetry raises two different but interlinked questions: one, what is a good life, morally speaking? and two, how should he relate to, and write about, the suffering, cruelty and injustice in the world around him? With a few exceptions, moral and political issues do not figure prominently in the poems in the first three collections. A change becomes apparent in the third, *Wintering Out* (1972), but it is only in *North* (1975) that moral or political problems emerge centrally in Seamus Heaney's writing: 'I shouldered a kind of manhood / stepping in to lift the coffins / of dead relations' ('Funeral Rites'). Violence in

Northern Ireland was at its height, Seamus Heaney and his family had moved to the South, responsibilities and choices were unavoidable. The following collections through the 1980s are much occupied with these responsibilities and choices. *Seeing Things* (1991) shows a lightening of mood although even this cheerful collection is framed by two translations describing descents to the world of the dead. *The Spirit Level* (1996) is balanced, neither resolutely cheerful nor preoccupied with heavy moral burdens.

The first question of a 'good life' is considered and reconsidered throughout the poetry. Much of what has been said in previous sections is very relevant: fidelity to place and people of his upbringing, appreciation of a range of experiences, an intelligent awareness of historical shapings, the relativity of one's own sensations but also the sharing of situations. Education, travel, work, religion, art, all offer certain possibilities but in none of these does Seamus Heaney exclusively locate his notion of a good life. Indeed, although there is much appreciation for people, affectionate portraits of his parents and love poems, there is a striking absence of heroes. Skills are respected, the independence of the fisherman in 'Casualty' is acknowledged, but it is hard to find a figure who can stand as a model. Two cases that could be advanced as exceptions are significant in their ordinariness. The shopkeeper in section VII of 'Station Island' is described as 'the perfect, clean, unthinkable victim' but Seamus Heaney is primarily remembering him as a footballer and a 'big-limbed, decent' person. The individual, from all the poetry, singled out for praise is his brother Hugh in 'Keeping Going'. Even here, Hugh is presented as a figure of fun and 'good stamina' rather than as a saint or a champion. 'Keeping going' is a kind of heroism in times of atrocity and instant solutions, 'But you [Hugh] cannot make the dead walk or right wrong'. In 'The Haw Lantern' the berry defies winter and provides 'a small light for small people'. Seamus Heaney speaks of keeping 'self-respect from dying out' rather than an illumination. He goes on to see the berry in another light and compares it to the Greek Cynic philosopher Diogenes who, according to legend, walked the streets of Athens carrying a lantern in broad daylight and claimed that he was trying to find one honest man. The poem reflects back on the elusiveness of such an honest man in Seamus Heaney's own poetry.

The second question concerns Seamus Heaney's response to the political struggles and violence, particularly in Northern Ireland. He has always been explicit about his upbringing in a Roman Catholic, nationalist community and, in 1983, issued 'An Open Letter' to the editors of *Contemporary British Verse* in which he was included as a British poet:

> be advised
> My passport's green [Irish].
> No glass of ours was ever raised
> To toast *The Queen*.

Although he was an active participant in the Civil Rights movement in the late 1960s, he has not given any public endorsement to a political party and he is not a practising Catholic. He has been branded by some Unionist politicians as an apologist for Republicanism, and castigated by Republicans as a traitor to Nationalism. In 'The Flight Path' he recalls how he was confronted in a train in 1979 by a fanatical Republican who demanded: '"When, for fuck's sake, are you going to write / Something for us?"' This was the same man who had years earlier 'in a dream' asked Seamus Heaney to drive a car bomb to its target at a border crossing. The poet as a person has obviously experienced over the years rage, sympathy, hatred, hope, fear, despair, thrill, horror, weariness, impotence, forgiveness, understanding, incomprehension; and such emotions occur in the poetry. As a poet, he has tried to write good poems involving these events and his responses to them. The poems will be looked at in five main groups.

MYTHICAL AND HISTORICAL PARALLELS

In his lecture 'Feeling into Words' (1974) published in *Preoccupations*, Seamus Heaney speaks of how his poetry had to change in response to the outbreak of sectarian violence in 1969: 'From that moment the problems of poetry moved from being simply a matter of achieving the satisfactory verbal icon to being a search for **images** and symbols adequate to our predicament' (*Preoccupations*, p. 56). In 1969 he read Glob's *The Bog People* (see Commentary on 'The Tollund Man') and in the descriptions of sacrificial killings in it he found what he felt were adequate images and symbols. Beginning with 'The Tollund Man', he wrote a series of bog poems in which he comments obliquely on the atrocities in Northern Ireland by relating them to brutal rituals in Nordic communities two thousand years earlier. Most of these poems are grouped together in *North* (1975) and the book's title includes both the north of Ireland and the north of Europe. The bog poems have certainly captivated readers but perhaps the tactic of distancing the events from immediate reaction and seeing them in a perspective of very different times, cultures and religions is too self-conscious; perhaps there is too much of the 'artful voyeur' ('Punishment'). In 'Funeral Rites' Seamus Heaney declares:

> Now as news comes in
> of each neighbourly murder
> we pine for ceremony,
> customary rhythms

He proposes a national funeral of the victims in the great Bronze Age burial chamber of New Grange, which happens to be very close to where the Battle of the Boyne was fought, and this ceremony will lay the whole troubled past to rest once and for all. 'Neighbourly murder', however, may require a more local, intimate answer and this is what we hear in the second group of poems.

FACING THE HORROR
The final few poems in *North* and half a dozen poems in the first half of *Field Work* (1979) show a shift away from the **mythic**, depersonalising method. Victims of killings are named, places are pinpointed, personal connections are established and the language is more direct and colloquial, often, indeed, using politicians' slogans and journalists' headlines with cutting **irony**. The violence is presented with a shocking immediacy: 'A pointblank teatime bullet' ('A Postcard from North Antrim' – in *Field Work*) and even when Seamus Heaney is away from the action he cannot escape from the reverberations. In 'Summer 1969' while horrifying events ravage Belfast he is in the Prado Museum in Madrid but what he sees there is Goya's famous painting of the execution of rebels and his terrifying series of depictions of violence: 'that holmgang / Where two berserks club each other to death / For honour's sake, greaved in a bog, and sinking'. 'Holmgang' is a small island where duellists fight

to the death; the image is painfully appropriate to the situation in Ireland. Through these poems a question about responsibility continues and some of his friends have clear and absolute views. Defensively, in a poem suitably titled 'Exposure', he replies: 'I am neither internee nor informer; / An inner émigré … a wood-kerne / Escaped from the massacre'. 'Inner émigré' is a phrase used of dissidents in the Soviet Union who remained in the country; and 'wood-kernes' are rebels in seventeenth-century Ireland who operated from the security of the forests. Seamus Heaney is engaged in a struggle but at a remove, as an artist.

CONSCIENCE AND SELF-INTERROGATION

The sequence called 'Station Island' (see note on page 37) presents a series of dramatic interrogations of Seamus Heaney with regard to his moral and artistic behaviour. In the second half of section VIII he is accused by his murdered cousin of having written falsely about his death: 'You saw that, and you wrote that – not the fact. / You confused evasion and artistic tact'. He claims that Seamus Heaney's poem, 'The Strand at Lough Beg', 'whitewashed ugliness' and 'saccharined my death'. The poetic pilgrimage, like the real one in Donegal, is an enterprise in penitence and self-assessment so that the now familiar questions are posed again but in the different terms of the encounters with dead friends and fellow Irish writers. Lightheaded with the strange ritual, lack of food and sleep, consciousness comes and goes, 'I dreamt and drifted'. A sense of 'connivance and mistrust', of being simultaneously 'biddable and unforthcoming' (section IX), disgusts him. In the end, he is released by the James Joyce figure who advises him to move beyond guilt and worry and go his own way: 'Keep at a tangent' (section XII).

DISTANCE GIVES PERSPECTIVE

Although *Sweeney Astray* was published some months before *Station Island*, I wish to consider it with 'Sweeney Redivivus', the third section of *Station Island*, as part of the same poetic effort and the next stage in Seamus Heaney's thinking on the social role of the artist. Seamus Heaney felt an affinity with Sweeney (see above, page 38) as a figure rebellious to religious and secular orthodoxies, gifted as a poet, and licensed by his 'madness' to be free from authority or predictability. The translation reads very empathetically and the wildness of the poem and its hero allows Seamus Heaney to imagine outrageously and write accordingly with abandon and gusto. The poems in 'Sweeney Redivivus' (remade) are the poet's own but very much in the spirit of Sweeney. They take risks and escape any tendency to timidity or circumspection to which he earlier thought himself prone:

> I was mired in attachment
> until they began to pronounce me
> a feeder off battlefields
>
> so I mastered new rungs of air
> to survey out of reach ('The First Flight')

'Drifting Off' describes this new bravado in terms of comparisons with other birds. In 'The Cleric' Seamus Heaney, as Sweeney, concludes that the pressures in the end: 'opened my path to a kingdom / of such scope and neuter allegiance / my emptiness reigns at its whim'.

MORAL PARABLES

This discovered freedom allows him to write a group of moral-political parables or allegories in *The Haw Lantern* (1987). The titles of the poems announce their symbolic nature: 'From the Frontier of Writing', 'Parable Island', 'From the Republic of Conscience', 'From the Land of the Unspoken', 'From the Canton of Expectation', 'The Mud Vision', 'The Disappearing Island'. There are no specific references to places or events in Ireland or elsewhere. The poems read like reports from explorers of unusual but recognisable human experience. They are not **mythic** in the manner of the bog poems but are visionary and curiously outside ordinary time. The individual, the poet, is granted an insight which is really a recognition of what he already knows or should know: 'Our unspoken assumptions have the force / of revelation' ('From the Land of the Unspoken' – in *The Haw Lantern*).

TECHNIQUES

VERSE

As is apparent from his collections of essays, Seamus Heaney is passionately interested in the craft of poetry. He writes with generous acknowledgement of a wide variety of poets as models and facilitators for his own practice. His translations from other poets have enabled him to experiment in **verse** forms and varieties of language not native to his own poetry. The range has included the Ancient Greek of Sophocles, the Latin of Virgil, the Old English of *Beowulf,* the Italian of Dante, the Polish of Jan Kochenowski, the Spanish of St John of the Cross, the Irish of various poets, and many poets of the twentieth century in different languages. From his earliest poems in the 1960s, the writing has always been self-conscious and carefully rehearsed; he has never been one for blurting or babbling.

Across his work, verse is seldom free. Behind what looks like **free verse** there is often a measured tread of **stresses**; and **rhyme**, when we don't think we hear it, is often lurking, even in unusual patterns or incomplete rhyme-sounds. There are complex **alliterative** and **assonantal** connections which give the verse a thickness of aural texture. He enjoys experimenting with different **stanza** forms; for example, in 'Mycenae Lookout' the five sections have each a distinct form, and 'Two Lorries' is in the unusual form of a **sestina**. He is particularly fond of a three-line unit, with or without rhyme, version of **terza rima**. In *North* (1975), very obviously, he adopts a short line of two or three stresses as if to make the difficulty of some of these poems more digestible. There are only a few **sonnets**, including 'Requiem for the Croppies', before *Field Work* (1979) and its ten 'Glanmore Sonnets'. The other concentrations of sonnets are the eight 'Clearances' written in memory of his mother and the series of eight in 'Glanmore Revisited'. He plays with different rhyme schemes and internal divisions in his sonnets, giving the traditional form his twist. In *Seeing Things* (1991) a new **verse** form appears. Under the general title of 'Squarings', forty-eight twelve-line, unrhymed poems are gathered in four groupings with twelve poems in each. Each poem is built of four **triplets**. The poems have a square look on the page but they have a playful, quirky feel to them. In 'Lightnings' number III the name is explained:

> Squarings? In the game of marbles, squarings
> Were all those anglings, aimings, feints and squints
> You were allowed before you'd shoot

Twenty years earlier Seamus Heaney experimented with **prose** poems. His collection *Stations* published in 1975 consists of twenty-one pieces, each about half a page in length, each trying to catch a moment or an incident in his upbringing. *Sweeney Astray* (1982) moves between verse and prose and one section of the poem 'The King of the Ditchbacks' is in prose.

As his career has progressed the sequence poem has exerted an increased fascination. A 'sequence poem' is one consisting of different parts juxtaposed without any connecting narrative. The strength of such a poem is that a situation or question can be approached from different angles without a narrow orthodoxy and allowing for inconsistency or, at least, uncertainty. There is one sequence poem in *Death of a Naturalist* (1966); there are eighteen in *The Spirit Level* (1996).

LANGUAGE

In the poem 'Making Strange' the poet stands between two figures, one with 'his travelled intelligence', the other 'unshorn and bewildered'. The two represent different aspects of Seamus Heaney himself which he sometimes finds difficult to reconcile: the sophisticated, highly educated side and the rougher, peasant side. In the poem a voice urges him to 'Be adept and be dialect', to be both sophisticated and earthy. In the end he feels 'adept / at dialect' as if he has succeeded in reconciling the two aspects. The title alludes to the Formalist theory of Victor Shklovsky who claimed that poetic use of language makes the familiar into something newly discovered and strange. Seamus Heaney certainly has a gift of making the ordinary special, for example, poking about in wells ('Personal Helicon'), eating oysters ('Oysters'), peeling potatoes ('Clearances' 3), hailstones ('Hailstones'), an old sofa ('Sofa in the Forties'). In 'Hailstones' some of the images are ordinary: 'those brats of showers', 'like a ruler across the knuckles', 'foraging in the nettles'; but there is another kind of vocabulary: 'intimated and disallowed', 'truest foretaste of your aftermath', 'dilation'. The poem 'Hercules and Antaeus' is emblematic of the same division and struggle between Hercules, 'Sky-born and royal', full of thrust and ambitions and Antaeus, 'the mould-hugger', whose strength relies on physical contact with the earth.

Seamus Heaney's early popularity was gained with the physical immediacy and earthiness of his poetry. The poems of *Death of a Naturalist* (1966) are rooted in soil and clay and bog and growth, and the language is sensuous, particularly tactile: 'The cold smell of potato mould, the squelch and slap / Of soggy peat' ('Digging'). The Bog poems exploit a rich vocabulary of substances as if the fibres and tissues of bodies and earth are actually there in the lines: 'The cured wound / opens inwards to a dark / elderberry place' ('The Grauballe Man'). Sometimes a violence or brutality is pushed at us in the choice of words, as when he is describing a fanatical drummer on an Orange march: 'The pigskin's scourged until his knuckles bleed' ('Orange Drums, Tyrone, 1966'). **Dialect** words and unusual but very exact terms keep Seamus Heaney's poetry plugged into the local, the particular and the personally apprehended: words such as, '"och ochs" and "och hohs"', 'glar', 'dailigone', 'slabbering', 'shucked', 'plinkings', 'scrim'. Use of dialogue has often a similar effect of localising a situation. This thickly textured quality in the language continues throughout his poetry, even in the more allegorical poems in *The Haw Lantern* (1987).

Not so obvious in the early work but gradually developing and becoming intermixed with the Antaean, heavy vocabulary, is a Herculean or elevated choice of words. Sometimes the terms are drawn from a religious tradition: 'scapulars', 'penitential', 'aspersed', 'apotheosis'; sometimes they are elements in a cosmopolitan cultural knowledge: 'omphalos', 'sprezzatura', 'empery', 'retiarius', 'ocarina'. It is significant that when the reader comes on a translation of St John of the Cross in section XI of *Station Island* it is utterly obvious that the 'poem' is not by Seamus Heaney himself – it is too monotonal, too fixed, although there are several different images, in one kind of language. As his career has gone on, Seamus Heaney's poems have become more mixed: the **diction** is more variegated, the tones more shifting. There is an easier, more conversational quality to much of *Seeing Things* (1991) and *The Spirit Level* (1996). He takes more risks with his **syntax** and with switches from light-heartedness to seriousness. In 'Man and Boy' he can move within six lines from 'Blessed be the detachment of dumb love' to, quoting his father (describing a salmon jumping), '"As big as a wee pork pig by the sound of it"'. It is in the same poem that he declares: 'Blessed be down-to-earth! Blessed be highs'. Antaeus and Hercules are both accommodated.

PART FOUR

EXTENDED COMMENTARIES

POEM 1

'Sunlight' (first part of 'Mossbawn: Two Poems in Dedication for Mary Heaney') in *North* (1975)

Sunlight

There was a sunlit absence.
The helmeted pump in the yard
heated its iron,
water honeyed

in the slung bucket   5
and the sun stood
like a griddle cooling
against the wall

of each long afternoon.
So, her hands scuffled   10
over the bakeboard,
the reddening stove

sent its plaque of heat
against her where she stood
in a floury apron   15
by the window.

Now she dusts the board
with a goose's wing,
now sits, broad-lapped,
with whitened nails   20

and measling shins:
here is a space
again, the scone rising
to the tick of two clocks.

And here is love   25
like a tinsmith's scoop
sunk past its gleam
in the meal-bin.

In his individual collections Seamus Heaney arranges the poems with care so that the poems comment on each other. *North* consists of 'Mossbawn', as a kind of preface, and two unequal sections of poems. The poems in both sections are deeply involved in the terrifying situation in Northern Ireland in the early seventies: the poems in Part I relate that situation to a wider historical context and offer parallels between aspects of the present and the past; the poems in Part II tend to be more personal and contemporary. 'Mossbawn' stands aside from the violence and anxieties which preoccupy the volume but also offers a perspective on that preoccupation. 'Mossbawn' is the name of the farm where Seamus Heaney grew up (see *Preoccupations*, pp. 17–19 and pp. 35–6) and the two poems, 'Sunlight' and 'The Seed Cutters', are dedicated to his aunt Mary who lived with his family.

The two poems record the routine, unspectacular work on the farm. 'Sunlight' concerns domestic work; 'The Seed Cutters' concerns outdoor work. The former focuses on a solitary, specific person, a woman; the latter describes a group action by men. 'Sunlight' is full of warmth and a sense of enclosure but is written in uneven, unrhymed **quatrains**; 'The Seed Cutters' conveys a chilly and exposed atmosphere but is devised as a **sonnet**. They complement each other and emphasise the quiet endurance and cooperation of people in contrast to the rancour and animosity of the remainder of *North*. The 'in Dedication' of the title of the poems holds a solemnity, honouring and consecrating the people and work of his background.

The title of the first poem, 'Sunlight', seems curious in that the predominant location of the poem is inside a kitchen, nineteen of the twenty-eight lines are indoors. The opening line, a sentence of statement, 'There was a sunlit absence', is difficult and mysterious. The word 'there' could be just part of the verbal statement 'There was' or it could be an adverb of location. Perhaps a contrast is intended between 'there' (that place or then) and 'here' in lines 22 and 25 and 'now' in lines 17 and 19. Also, 'sunlit' is a physical word but 'absence' is an abstract word and the two do not fit easily together. Most of the vocabulary in the poem is physical: 'pump', 'hands', 'apron'; but the conclusion puts forward a large abstraction, 'love', perhaps intimated by lines 22–3: 'here is a space / again' which connects with 'absence'. Primarily, the 'absence' is an absence of people in the yard; the human activity is happening in the kitchen. In the mind of the poet, and he does not appear or intervene in the poem till the final **stanza**, the exterior and interior are simultaneous, parallel, and the link is made in the 'So' of line 10.

Although the yard is empty of people, the scene is bright and familiar (see *Preoccupations*, p. 17) with the pump, the bucket of water and the hot sun. Each of the three items has, however, an oddity in expression. The 'pump ... heated its iron' describes the metal warming in the sunshine but the transitive verb suggests that an implement is being deliberately heated up. The word 'honeyed' in line 4 is unusual as a verb but conveys very economically how the water takes on the warm, pale thickness of honey. The sun is likened in lines 6–9 to a 'griddle', a flat metal plate employed for baking on, left to cool down against the outside wall after being used. Such oddity in expression compels the reader's attention to the descriptions.

'Each long afternoon' gives the sense of repetition and routine. This sense is picked up in the 'So' which marks the shift indoors and to the activity of a person. With her hands she is mixing the ingredients to prepare a scone for baking; 'scuffled' suggests the irregular movements as she adjusts to the texture of the mixture. The fierce heat of the stove, probably an open range, is given a solidity against her body in the word 'plaque', like a large branding iron. Each part of the process is unhurried, routine: 'Now she dusts ... now sits'. The poem has shifted into the present tense as if the preparation is finished and we await the results. Aunt Mary sits, her nails full of flour, her bare shins blotched red by the stove's heat, and waits for the scone to cook. Like the 'absence' in line 1, the 'space' in line 22 is not an emptiness but a different part of the whole process. The 'two clocks' may be actual clocks or the two dimensions of presence and absence.

The afternoon has passed, the scone is rising to completion, and the final stanza has the feel of a logical deduction or conclusion: 'There was' ... 'So' ... 'Now' ... 'And here is love'. The final stanza is the only time in the poem when a stanza coincides with a whole sentence. Generally through the poem, lines have two or three main **stresses** but without regularity. The final stanza reads in a measured way with sound repetitions connecting 'here', 'glean' and 'meal', and 'is', 'tinsmith's', 'its', 'in' and 'bin'. The question is: how does the statement of the stanza fit with the rest of the poem? The **image** of the scoop (a small curved shovel made by tinkers or travelling people) buried almost out of sight in the meal-bin is one of lavishness and generosity. The meal-bin looks back to the aunt's scone-making; and 'sunk past its gleam' echoes the 'sunlit absence' of the opening line and the colour of the honeyed water. 'And here is love' does connect with the warm, affectionate feel of the poem but it is also an assertion of faith or validation: what is durable and cherishable is there in the ordinary farm of his upbringing and that love stands against or beyond the strife described in the following poems in *North*.

POEM *2*

'The First Flight' in *Station Island* (1984)

The First Flight

It was more sleepwalk than spasm
yet that was a time when the times
were also in spasm –

the ties and the knots running through us
split open   5
down the lines of the grain.

As I drew close to pebbles and berries,
the smell of wild garlic, relearning
the acoustic of frost

and the meaning of woodnote,   10
my shadow over the field
was only a spin-off,

my empty place an excuse
for shifts in the camp, old rehearsals
of debts and betrayal.   15

Singly they came to the tree
with a stone in each pocket
to whistle and bill me back in

and I would collide and cascade
through leaves when they left,   20
my point of repose knocked askew.

I was mired in attachment
until they began to pronounce me
a feeder off battlefields

so I mastered new rungs of the air   25
to survey out of reach
their bonfires on hills, their hosting

and fasting, the levies from Scotland
as always, and the people of art
diverting their rhythmical chants   30

to fend off the onslaught of winds
I would welcome and climb
at the top of my bent.

This is the sixth poem in the sequence 'Sweeney Redivivus' (Sweeney Recreated) and is written in the **persona** of Sweeney (see Commentaries on pages 38, 43, 68). The word 'persona' derives from the Latin term for a mask worn by an actor in a play; such a mask disguises the actor and also enables him to act in the character represented by the mask. When a poet creates and writes in a persona, it is not possible for the reader to be certain which aspects belong to the poet as a person and which to the devised character. Based on medieval accounts of the legendary seventh-century Irish King Sweeney, the persona in 'Sweeney Redivivus' allows Seamus Heaney to sound more extravagant, 'madder' than he is in ordinary life. Using the persona of an accursed, paranoid poet-king, gifted with an ability to fly, Seamus Heaney can not be held responsible for the thoughts expressed: there is an insulating, dramatic space between the words and the author.

Nonetheless, and, of course, Seamus Heaney did write the poems, something of the poet and his situation can be discerned. The title itself allows several interpretations. 'Flight' can be a cowardly or defeatist running-away from a difficulty. It can also be, and particularly in the case of a 'first flight', a new, exhilarating launch into the air. A third sense could be, as in the phrase 'a flight of fancy', an exercise in ingenuity or imagination. Connecting with 'rungs' (line 25), it could suggest a section of stairs, a crucial stage in his development. The first two interpretations appear to be the most operative in the poem and fit with the source of Sweeney's story (see Seamus Heaney's *Sweeney Astray*, sections 13–18, 1982). Seamus Heaney, however, who had worked on his translation in the ten years since his 'flight' from Northern Ireland to the Republic in 1972, suggests a fuller reading of the Sweeney figure: 'It is possible to read the work as an aspect of the quarrel between free creative imagination and the constraints of religious, political and domestic obligation' (*Sweeney Astray*, p. viii).

The poem is written in three-line units but without a set length of line or **rhyme**. Although there is no fixed **metre**, a number of lines, particularly in the final **stanzas**, seem to slip into an **anapaestic rhythm** (two unstressed syllables followed by a stressed syllable) which gives a springing movement to the **verse**. The thirty three lines are arranged in only four sentences, of uneven length and very different **syntactic** shape; the sentences so often crossing the gaps between **triplets** give a sense of transcending local obstacles, and the final sentence is the most sustained leap, the most exciting flight. Twenty four of the thirty three lines have no terminal punctuation, again showing a momentum carrying the poem across boundary lines, and again this impetus is most obvious in the final sentence. These formal developments fit with a shift in the mood of the speaker, from the passivity of 'sleepwalk' in line 1 to the assertion of 'mastered' in line 25 and the very positive final lines.

The Sweeney-Heaney narrator lives in troubled times and the turmoil or 'spasm' is in the speaker and in the situation around him (note the 'also' in line 3). Conveying the breakdown in society, the **metaphors** in the second stanza are themselves confused. Associations and groupings ('ties and the knots') which had developed in the community break apart and a more basic alignment of traditional loyalties is reasserted, just as a length of wood will split along its natural grain and exclude the cross-grained knots where branches had grown. The escape from this violent struggle, however, seems curiously automatic, a 'sleepwalk', rather than the result of a conscious, dramatic decision. Once out of the turmoil, Sweeney-Heaney takes a therapeutic pleasure in the simple things of the natural world, attending to reading that world through his senses. The line 'the acoustic of frost' catches the clean, brittle breaking of frost underfoot and also the altered acoustics when frost has tightened its hold on water and vegetation. In the archaic 'woodnote' a lost lore of the countryside is suggested and 'relearning ... the meaning of woodnote' has a subtlety and calm knowledge far removed from the earlier convulsive 'spasm'. And, in comparison with this healing simplicity, the aspects of his new life more obvious to others seem unimportant to him: his ability to fly is a mere 'spin-off' and his absence from his customary public position simply a subject for rumour and recrimination among his acquaintances. The feuds, antagonisms and accusations continue as before but he feels released from involvement in them.

Not that he is allowed total peace. His acquaintances track him down and try to threaten or cajole him back into line with what they see as his tribal responsibility. They launch stones of accusation at his refuge in a tree or try to flatter him to rejoin them. 'Bill' can mean 'enrol' as in a club or army, or make courting gestures as in birds' 'billing and cooing'. They can still upset him and make his life uncomfortable but a special accusation drives him away from all contact with them. Some sense of responsibility still lurked in him: 'I was mired in attachment'; perhaps Seamus Heaney's use of 'mired' recalls his early earthy poems and the Bog poems of *North* (1975) but 'mired' also contains an element of contamination. When he (the Heaney part of the narrator) was branded as a poetic cannibal whose poetry fed on the pain and deaths of the victims of violence, he could treat with his accusers no longer. The original Sweeney had, after the Battle of Moira in 637, been accused of slaying people excluded under the rules of combat. Like the legendary Sweeney who flew beyond the confines of his native territory, Seamus Heaney took off for the United States in 1982 and from then on has operated in international airways. The narrator has climbed the air above his detractors and above the squabbles in his homeplace. The final nine lines contain an ambivalence in that he does not ignore what goes on, he can still 'survey' the scene, but he relishes the challenge of new vistas. The main imagery in these lines takes its terms from an earlier period in Ireland's history, for example, the 'bonfires' and the 'rhythmical chants', but there is the frightening reflection that the terms can still apply in the Ulster of the 1980s with its sectarian rituals and shows of force. Bonfires are still lit, religious/political displays of fervour ('hosting' can mean raising an army as well as the sacrament), Scotland's Orange Order still sends 'representatives' ('levies') to Northern Ireland to demonstrate religious and military support at Protestant rallies. There are still elements of parochialism or even xenophobia in a nationalistic suspicion of foreign influence, the 'winds'. Sweeney-Heaney exults in facing newness and in riding the strange currents of air.

The poem has moved from the dull inevitable constraints of the opening to the daring and defiance of the ending; the poem is a kind of flight. Seamus Heaney is not detached from the cruelty and mechanical routines of the sectarian strife in his native Northern Ireland but he has aimed, as an artist, for a vantage point above the turmoil where different perspectives come into play. In using the **persona** of Mad Sweeney he has pushed himself to 'the top of my bent' or powers. There is, in the final phrase, an echo of Hamlet and his adopted madness (*Hamlet*, III.2.192), an echo perhaps already heard in 'the times were also in spasm' and Hamlet's: 'The time is out of joint. O cursed spite, / That ever I was born to set it right' (*Hamlet*, I.5.188–9). Seamus Heaney had already **ironically** employed this allusion to Hamlet's complaint in the penultimate line of 'Sandstone Keepsake', also in *Station Island*.

POEM 3

'Postscript' in *The Spirit Level* (1996)

Postscript

And some time make the time to drive out west
Into County Clare, along the Flaggy Shore,
In September or October, when the wind
And the light are working off each other
So that the ocean on one side is wild   5
With foam and glitter, and inland among stones
The surface of a slate-grey lake is lit
By the earthed lightning of a flock of swans,

> Their feathers roughed and ruffling, white on white,
> Their fully grown headstrong-looking heads   10
> Tucked or cresting or busy underwater.
> Useless to think you'll park and capture it
> More thoroughly. You are neither here nor there,
> A hurry through which known and strange things pass
> As big soft buffetings come at the car sideways   15
> And catch the heart off guard and blow it open.

The word 'postscript' is used of a passage added at the end of a piece of writing, in particular, of a note added to a letter after the signature of the writer. It suggests an afterthought or something that was missed out of the main text. This poem 'Postscript' comes at the end of the collection *The Spirit Level* but in what sense is the poem a postscript? Does it contain something missed out or neglected in the collection? Or does it contain an afterthought on elements in the collection? Some continuity with something earlier is indicated in the opening 'And'. The collection is very varied, with pain and anxiety as well as happy memories and good moments. The title, *The Spirit Level*, is not an unambiguous label. It could indicate a spiritual dimension as distinct from the physical world. It could refer to the instrument used by builders to ascertain the horizontal. It could point to equanimity, a balanced mood (where 'level' is an adjective). All three elements feature in the collection in different degrees. Perhaps 'Postscript' gives a final emphasis.

    The opening is relaxed and conversational: 'And some time make the time'; it is a recommendation to a friend who would appreciate the experience or perhaps to himself, not a command or matter of urgency. County Clare is on the west of Ireland with a long Atlantic coastline, big open skies, grey rock and a wonderful light. A time of year is specified so that the conditions will be right. What is being recommended is not a picturesque view or a specially colourful scene or a rare animal. In fact, the experience is simultaneously described in detail and peculiarly vague. The opening eleven lines offer circumstances and details but the point of the trip is left hanging as 'it' in line 12. Furthermore, the traveller is warned: 'Useless to think you'll park and capture it / More thoroughly'. In the final sentence the individual person is demoted as 'neither here nor there, / A hurry'. 'Here' and 'there' could be geographical or spiritual locations but the phrase 'neither here nor there' has a dismissive quality. To be called a 'hurry' is very belittling; we can never have a solid hold on the mystery but must be nomadic or a tourist. Nonetheless, the experience offered is worth travelling for and is enormous enough to 'catch the heart off guard and blow it open'. What is this experience, the 'it'?

The form of the poem contributes to what is proposed. The verse is a loose **blank verse**, usually with five stressed syllables in each line but the **stress** pattern thickens in the final lines as if something important is being consolidated. There is a flexibility in the verse, and without **rhyme** to mark the end of lines or punctuation to arrest the movement, the sense flows almost casually. There are only three sentences in the sixteen lines: a long opening sentence in which the scene is established, a short sentence of caution, and a final push impeded by only a single comma. We are carried along in an undemanding way till we hit 'it' in line 12 and realise that we have to go back because we were not attending closely enough. The 'off guard' in the final line is not the same as inattention.

Somehow, the ingredients in the long first sentence must lead to the 'it'. A crucial phrase is 'working off' in line 4. 'Working off' is like 'playing off' in, for example, football where two players complement each other's strengths and produce a result which neither could manage singly. In the poem the wind and light in autumn combine to create special effects. The road runs along a sort of causeway between the expanse of the open sea and an inland lake. A contrast and a complementarity are established by the working off each other of the wind and light. The ocean is all agitation and 'glitter'; the lake is, by comparison, dull and 'slate-grey' but takes colour and drama from the extraordinary brightness ('white on white') of the swans, caught in the lavish **image** of 'earthed lightning'. The swans go about their own business but their changing shapes are part of the transformation of the lake. In the wind, their soft neck-feathers are blown against how they naturally lie and look like ruffs or ruffled collars. Seamus Heaney's choice of words is very exact to the movements of the birds. In line 10 the repetition of 'head' seems clumsy at a first reading but the imperious gestures of swans are captured vividly. In 'headstrong-looking' Seamus Heaney packs details of the powerful necks, the sense of purpose, and the fierce eyes of the creatures. This force of the birds, a force of the air, is momentarily 'earthed' or tamed but also brings a fierce otherworldly power ('lightning') to the scene. The traditional four elements – earth, air, fire and water – are simultaneously present in a potent combination of 'known and strange'.

This combination has to be apprehended as it presents itself. It is not so much an aesthetic arrangement as an emotional revelation. Photographs would not hold it. We are incidental to such combinations but it is our transitory nature that responds to them. The 'big soft buffetings' are gusts of wind but have something of the quality of swans' wings taking off in flight. The human heart is what is susceptible to this mingling of 'known and strange' and there is a shock of illumination and enlargement. 'Blow it open' is enhancing not destructive. In this optimism, the poem as a 'postscript' stresses an admiration Seamus Heaney has shown in the collection for a quiet acceptance of the miraculous, of a mingling of the spirit level and the mundane. Talking about his ambitions in the collection, he said that he wished to write a poetry, 'Not registering the endured, but proffering the imagined' (BBC Radio Interview, May 1996).

PART FIVE

BACKGROUND

SEAMUS HEANEY

Seamus Heaney was born in 1939 at Mossbawn in rural County Derry in Northern Ireland. His family had a small farm and his father was a cattle dealer. Educated in the local primary school, Seamus Heaney went away to school in Derry and then to Queen's University in Belfast. He taught in various schools and colleges including Queen's University. In Belfast he attended a poetry group organised by the poet and critic Philip Hobsbaum. He married Marie Devlin in 1965. His first collection *Death of a Naturalist* was published in 1966 by Faber and Faber, the leading publishers of poetry. His second collection *Door into the Dark* appeared in 1969 by which time the troubles in Northern Ireland had broken out. By the late 1960s he had been involved in the Civil Rights movements and the protests against the inherent injustice in the province.

After a year lecturing at the University of California at Berkeley he moved south to Glanmore, County Wicklow in 1972, the year of his third collection *Wintering Out*. 1972 was also the year of 'Bloody Sunday' in which thirteen Civil Rights marchers were shot by British soldiers in Derry and the violence increased. Over the next few years Seamus Heaney, living in Dublin, for a time worked as a lecturer, for a time worked as a freelance writer. In 1975 *North* appeared and in 1979 *Field Work*. His first collection of essays, *Preoccupations*, was published in 1980, the same year that Field Day was established (see below).

From 1982 till 1996 he spent part of his year in Harvard, where he became the Boylston Professor of Rhetoric and Poetry, and part back home in Dublin. 1983 saw the publication of his translation of the medieval Irish poem, *Sweeney Astray*, followed by *Station Island* in 1984. By then he had become the most celebrated poet in English and his readings attracted large audiences around the world. *The Haw Lantern* (1987) reflected this international appeal, in that many of the poems were not located specifically in Ireland. In 1986 he delivered the T.S. Eliot Memorial Lectures and these were published as *The Government of the*

Tongue in 1988. His one play, *The Cure at Troy*, based on a play by Sophocles, was produced in 1990.

From 1989 to 1994 he occupied the Chair of Poetry at Oxford and, in 1995, his lectures in Oxford were published as *The Redress of Poetry*. His poems *Seeing Things* were issued in 1991. He was awarded the Nobel Prize for literature in 1995 and in 1996 his collection *The Spirit Level* was published.

His public profile is remarkable for a poet. As a propagandist for poetry he is persuasive and tireless. Prizes, doctorates and attention by the media have not dislodged his approachability or his genial decency and common sense.

HISTORICAL BACKGROUND

Because so many of Seamus Heaney's poems relate to a specifically Irish situation, it is useful to have some knowledge of the events in Irish history which have fed into the present situation. The old province of Ulster, from which modern Northern Ireland derives, was always somewhat at odds with the other parts of Ireland. The mythological/legendary period of Ulster around two thousand years ago hardly appears in Seamus Heaney's work. He probably deliberately avoided material and figures such as Cuchulainn, the great warrior, and Deirdre, the fated beauty, because they had been so heavily exploited by W.B. Yeats. Christianity, associated with St Patrick, arrived in Ireland in the fifth century and flourished in its individual Celtic form. Viking raids and settlements took place between the eighth and the eleventh centuries and Norse place names still bear testimony to the influence of the Vikings. In the twelfth century Norman-English were invited into Ireland as military allies but the military campaigns developed into systematic occupation of substantial parts of Ireland including areas in Ulster. The English language was introduced into many aspects of public life.

In the sixteenth century strenuous efforts were exerted by the English monarchs, particularly Elizabeth, to quell dissident Irish chiefs. The Protestant Reformation which led to England's independence from Roman Catholicism took little hold in Ireland, and Ireland came to be viewed as a potential ally of Catholic France and Spain, the enemies of

England. Ulster posed a particular threat because of its close links with some of the Catholic, Gaelic-speaking clans in north-west Scotland, and King James VI of Scotland who became James I of the United Kingdoms in 1603, decided on a drastic policy of introducing mainly Lowland Scottish, mainly Presbyterian, families into Ulster to form an ethnic, religious barrier to thwart the Celtic threat. These human plantations continued through the seventeenth century and extended throughout Ireland particularly after Oliver Cromwell's military conquest of the country. King William of Orange's victory at the Battle of the Boyne in 1690 gave power to the Anglo-Irish Protestants over the native Irish Catholics; this power was enforced for the following century through the Penal laws which operated against Presbyterian and Non-Conformists as well as Catholics. Disputes in Ulster between Catholic and Presbyterian landowners and landworkers led in 1795 to the formation of the Orange Order which protected the interests of Presbyterians and commemorated the Williamite victory at the Boyne on 12 July each year in parades through 'their' territory with flute and lambeg-drum bands.

In 1798 a series of uprisings took place across Ireland, protesting against or in favour of different policies in the various parts of Ireland. Some risings were republican, following the French Revolution; some were aimed at emancipation of Catholics. Many of the leaders in Ulster and elsewhere were Protestant, including Wolfe Tone. The Act of Union abolished the separate Irish Parliament in 1800 and the risings were defeated, despite some French help, by 1803. The rule of the Anglo-Irish or Ascendancy was strengthened although the Penal laws were gradually relaxed and Catholics were allowed to stand for Parliament after 1829. The population of Ireland grew steadily till the 1840s when a blight ruined the potato crop, the staple diet, in several successive years. Perhaps one million people died of starvation and disease, and a massive emigration in the same period further depleted the population. The failure or refusal of the British Government to intervene aggravated the bitterness and despair of the Irish and fuelled further sporadic acts of insurrection and violence. In 1916, when Britain was engaged in the First World War, public buildings in central Dublin were occupied by armed rebels. The Easter Rising was crushed by the British Army and fifteen of its leaders were executed after a brief secret military trial. In 1922 a settlement was reached by which part of Ulster with a large Protestant majority would remain as part of the United Kingdom and the remainder would become a separate entity, the Irish Free State. The divisions and bloodshed in the years between 1916 and 1923, including a civil war, and the partition of the island have not proved a good basis for a peaceful and contented Ireland.

Resentment by Catholics in Northern Ireland at unfair allocation of resources in housing, education, employment and culture led to the growth of a Civil Rights movement in the 1960s supported by some Protestants. The clashes between agitators and the authorities came to a violent head in 1969 and a subsequent increase in activity of para-military groups on both sides of the sectarian divide. Thousands of people have been killed on both sides, prominent figures have been assassinated, soldiers and policemen have been ambushed, and bombings by the IRA in England have caused huge destruction and many deaths. Republicans in prison for terrorist crimes went on hunger strike in 1981 and ten starved to death. The brutality has been extraordinary over a generation in which children now grown-up have never known anything but the Troubles. Since 1994 various new efforts were made to establish a lasting cease-fire and in 1998 an inter-party agreement was signed by the main groups of Unionists and Nationalists.

LITERARY BACKGROUND

Seamus Heaney's family background was not bookish and, outside school, he developed his reading through comics and boys' adventure stories. Folk songs, ballads and verse narrative recitations were standard elements in communal entertainment. The school syllabus consisted of standard English texts which he read dutifully rather than enthusiastically. In the opening three essays in *Preoccupations* (1980) he describes some aspects of the process by which he eventually arrived at an enjoyment of language and a dabbling in writing: 'The first book I remember owning and cherishing ... was Robert Louis Stevenson's *Kidnapped* ... I sat up all night to finish Thomas Hardy's *Return of the Native*'. Although he obviously enjoyed much of the reading required for his Degree in English at Belfast, he appears to have had no special inclination to write poetry till about 1962 when he was twenty three.

Philip Hobsbaum, an English poet and critic, arrived in Belfast to lecture in Queen's University and set up a small writing group which included Seamus Heaney, his wife-to-be Marie Devlin, Seamus Deane, Michael Longley and James Simmons. Seamus Heaney has credited the open atmosphere of those weekly sessions and the encouraging guidance of Hobsbaum with bringing something literary out of him and giving him a confidence in his own poetry. It was when, as a student, he read the poetry of Gerard Manley Hopkins that he first thought of writing himself and his early work shows the influence of Hopkins and Ted Hughes. He was aware that his literary education had been mainly in the English tradition and it did not quite match his Irish experience. In an essay in 1972 he wrote: 'I speak and write in English, but do not altogether share the preoccupations and perspectives of an Englishman. I teach English literature, I publish in London, but the English tradition is not ultimately home. I live off another hump as well' (*Preoccupations*, p. 34). As a school-boy he had gone to learn Irish in Irish-speaking areas in Donegal and his education in and attachment to the Irish tradition would grow steadily over the years and feed into his poetry. When he read the poetry of Patrick Kavanagh (1904–67), he recognised, for the first time, a voice speaking from his own background. From subsistence farming in County Monaghan, Kavanagh knew the sour, ingrown, unromantic life in rural Ireland. *The Great Hunger* (1942), a long poem, shows Paddy Maguire's meagre existence, spiritually deadened by three maternal forces: Mother Earth, Mother Church and his old domineering mother. Although Seamus Heaney did not share Kavanagh's grim vision, he knew where Kavanagh came from and he felt that the older poet empowered and gave a voice to a neglected, inarticulate side of Ireland, related to Seamus Heaney's own reticent, undemonstrative community where 'Whatever you say, you say nothing'. Kavanagh denounced the romantic, Celtic Twilight, heroic Ireland, invented, he claimed, by Yeats and his Anglo-Irish friends in the Celtic Revival at the turn of the century. Seamus Heaney, however, has always seen Yeats as a supreme poet and, for his own development, he learned from both. Yeats's commitment to the high calling of poetry, his huge sweep of thought, verbal density and 'passionate syntax' (Yeats's phrase), have served as a model to Seamus Heaney. Yeats died in 1939, the year of Seamus Heaney's birth. A con-temporary of Kavanagh, Louis MacNeice represents an entirely different stance but, in his very difference, has been instructive to Seamus Heaney. MacNeice was born in Belfast, his father became a bishop in the Church of Ireland (Anglican), he was sent, when his mother died, to a school in England and spent most of his life there but felt Irish in some confused sense. MacNeice's gift as a craftsman and his ambivalent feelings about identity, national and otherwise, have afforded Seamus Heaney an other perspective on some of his problems. Each of these poets, Yeats, Kavanagh, MacNeice, had to sort out his allegiance to the claims of different traditions in culture and in writing, and each aligned himself individually. Seamus Heaney's own alignment is specific to himself.

It is symptomatic of his disregard for compartments, national or otherwise, and his open-minded, energetic participation in several projects simultaneously that from the early eighties to the mid nineties he should have been enthusiastically involved in the Field Day Group in Ireland and a teacher at Harvard for half of each year. Field Day, made up of artists and intellectuals, sought, from its base in Derry, to promote the discussion of issues in Irish cultural awareness through plays, lectures, pamphlets and poetry. The focus was Irish but the perspectives were international and multi-cultural. Over the same period at Harvard, Seamus Heaney taught an inclusive range of poets, Irish, British, North American, East European or whatever. Many of these poets in turn had some influence on his own writing or his awareness as a writer. Perhaps his interest in the East European poets needs an explanation in that he could read them only in translation. In the introductory chapter to his essays *The Government of The Tongue* (1988) he writes:

> In the course of this book, Mandelstam and other poets from Eastern bloc
> countries are often invoked. I keep returning to them because there is something in
> their situation that makes them attractive to a reader whose formative experience
> has been largely Irish. There is an unsettled aspect to the different worlds they
> inhabit, and one of the challenges they face is to survive amphibiously, in the realm
> of 'the times' and the realm of their moral and artistic self-respect, a challenge
> immediately recognizable to anyone who has lived with the awful and demeaning
> facts of Northern Ireland's history over the last couple of decades. (p. xx)

The poets he has in mind would include, apart from Osip Mandelstam, Zbigniew Herbert, Czeslaw Milosz, Miroslav Holub, Joseph Brodsky, Anna Akhmatova and Boris Pasternak.

His appreciation of fellow poets is manifest in the eclectic nature of his choice of subjects for his Oxford lectures: Hugh MacDiarmid, John Clare, Elizabeth Bishop and Brian Merriman are not obvious poetic companions. He has been consistently generous in his praise of contemporaries such as Robert Lowell, Norman MacCaig, Derek Walcott, Stevie Smith, Sorley MacLean, Sylvia Plath, Philip Larkin and Ted Hughes. He happens to be an Irish poet and that complicated fact is important to him but his vision of poetry and the function of a poet for his or her audience is not circumscribed by nationality, religion or language.

For him there is nothing strange in acknowledging a poetic debt to the Italian Dante (1265–1321), the English Shakespeare (1564–1616), the Irish Eoghan Rua O Suilleabhain (1748–84) and the American Robert Frost (1874–1963). His modesty with his peers is unusual, his ambition for poetry is, even with his doubts, very high:

> Faced with the brutality of the historical onslaught, they [poetry and the imaginative arts] are practically useless. Yet they verify our singularity, they strike and stake out the ore of self which lies at the base of every individuated life. In one sense the efficacy of poetry is nil – no lyric has ever stopped a tank. In another sense, it is unlimited. It is like the writing in the sand in the face of which accusers and accused are left speechless and renewed. (*The Government of the Tongue*, p. 107)

And:

> We go to poetry, we go to literature in general, to be forwarded within ourselves. The best it can do is give us an experience that is like foreknowledge of certain things which we already seem to be remembering. What is at work in this most original and illuminating poetry is the mind's capacity to conceive a new plane of regard for itself, a new scope for its own activity. (*The Redress of Poetry*, pp. 159–60)

PART SIX

CRITICAL HISTORY & FURTHER READING

There are more than twenty books devoted to Seamus Heaney's work and hundreds of articles and chapters have been written on him. His extraordinary popularity has itself caused critics to examine the nature of his success and provoked some to challenge the basis of such a success. Outlined below are some of the critical approaches to his poetry; examples can be found most easily in *The Poetry of Seamus Heaney*, edited by Elmer Andrews, Icon Critical Guides, 1998 (see Further Reading).

POETRY AS POETRY

Some critics see poetry as a unique kind of utterance, in the discussion of which content, the thoughts expressed, cannot be properly or fully analysed in detachment from the specific poetic form and arrangements of language peculiar to that poem. This approach is in general agreement with the emphasis of New Criticism, a fashion of literary study developed in the 1920s and 1930s which achieved an orthodoxy in the teaching of literature by the 1950s and 1960s, but would not isolate a literary text from its social or historical context in the way sometimes done by the New Critics. Sensuous or intellectual enjoyment and a sense of imaginative enlargement in the reader would be seen as fundamental to a wish to write about poetry, and the ambition of the critic would be to open out the workings of the text to show how effects are created in the reader. Seamus Heaney's own essays on other poets move along similar lines where he offers parallel and sympathetic commentaries on how the poetry works on and in his mind.

Examples of such writers on Seamus Heaney include Helen Vendler (1995) and John Carey (in the *Sunday Times*, 1979–96). Both share their excitement and involvement in the poems and write perceptively on how the poems function as linguistic entities. Their admiration, while not unquestioning, is everywhere apparent and they present Seamus Heaney as a very special poet grappling with the difficulties of thinking out and exploring in the peculiar arrangements of words which are poetry the pleasures and pains and contradictions of his existence in a particular social context at a particular time. Such approving critics draw attention to his powers of observation, his gift for a phrase which seems surprising but absolutely accurate, the variety of subject matter, his versatility with verse forms, his presentation of complex moral issues, the balance between passion and restraint, the sense of troubled decency, the affection for his world. Bernard O'Donoghue (1994) offers a more technical linguistic analysis of verbal patterns in the poetry. An advantage of the approach described in this paragraph lies in its close working with what is actually there on the page; a possible weakness is in an obedience or submissive attitude which suggests an inbred, complicit relationship between poet and critic.

SOCIOLOGICAL AND POLITICAL READINGS

Poetry has always been seen as reflecting and commenting on the society in which it is written. Sometimes the relation of a poem to its social context seems obvious, sometimes a connection is less clear. Elements of the language itself (diction, grammar and syntax) may locate the composition in a period of history or a section of society. Over the past two decades or so a considerable deal of criticism has been written by people who see literary studies as an aspect of cultural studies; hence, analyses of literary texts may see them as manifestations of ideological positions rather than as literary artefacts. In the case of Seamus Heaney, this 'cultural' approach has been intensified by two factors: one, his Northern Irish upbringing and the situation there have imposed certain burdens on his poetry; and, two, the traditions of Irish literature and nationalism are ever present and ever pressing on an Irish writer.

IRISH IDENTITY AND NATIONALISM

For many readers, Seamus Heaney, the most anthologised poet of his generation, is the representative figure of modern Irish literature. His international recognition has placed him in a special position to speak for his country. He appears in his writing and in his public performances as unbitter, unpartisan, conciliatory, reasonable, inclusive. It is precisely to these qualities that some of his critics take exception. David Lloyd in an essay '"Pap for the Dispossessed": Seamus Heaney and the Poetics of Identity' (1985) denounces the balanced poetry: 'The unpleasantness of such poetry lies in the manner in which contradictions between the ethical and aesthetic elements in the writing are easily resolved by the subjugation of the former to the latter in the interests of producing the "well-made-poem"'. Edna Longley makes a similar point about Seamus Heaney's use of myth in *North* even if her viewpoint is different from that of Lloyd. According to both of them, Seamus Heaney's tactic of commenting on contemporary sectarian killings by relating them to ritual executions two thousand years earlier fudges the actuality of violence in a specific community. Some critics accuse Seamus Heaney of writing poetry subservient to a Nationalist ideology; others denounce him for betraying his background and not being sufficiently condemnatory of British injustice. In 1991 Desmond Fennell launched a savage attack on Seamus Heaney's reputation in a pamphlet, *Whatever You Say Say Nothing: Why Seamus Heaney is No.1*. This presents Seamus Heaney as having sold his Irish heritage in exchange for British and American academic acceptance, a kind of internationally marketable package.

GENDER AND RELIGION

Seamus Heaney's use of myth and imagery drawn from the Irish tradition has also brought a reprimand from Clair Wills who feels that he has indulged in a stereotyped representation of Ireland as female, intuitive and powerless in contrast to colonial England as masculine, rational and dominating. Elizabeth Cullingford has taken exception to what she sees as the poet's unquestioning use of female personifications of Ireland as Kathleen Ni Houlihan or Mother Ireland to perpetuate a notion of gender attributes: female as pure and passive, male as all powerful. Similar critiques have been made of his exploitation of religions imagery drawn from both paganism and his Roman Catholic background. The contention is that he is glibly validating certain traditional notions of spirituality when he should be querying the solidity and relevance of such concepts in the late twentieth and early twenty-first century.

I must add that some of the readings mentioned above seem to me to be extremely strained and, although the questions raised about Seamus Heaney's ideas and assumptions are intelligent and proper, many of the essays show a poor grasp of how poetry works and often operate with a very partial use of evidence. There *are* ambivalences, contradictions, revisions, uncertainties throughout Seamus Heaney's work but too many critics seem to wish to constrain him to follow a single line (their line) or take issue with an aspect of his poetry as if he has failed to notice any difficulty himself. The student should look out 'The Strand at Lough Beg' (*Field Work*) and Section VIII of 'Station Island', follow the debate carried through these poems, and ask the question: why does Seamus Heaney publish both poems?

FURTHER READING

Works by Seamus Heaney

Death of a Naturalist, Faber and Faber, 1966

Door into the Dark, Faber and Faber, 1969

Wintering Out, Faber and Faber, 1972

North, Faber and Faber, 1975

Field Work, Faber and Faber, 1979

Selected Poems 1965–1975, Faber and Faber, 1980

Preoccupations: Selected Prose 1968–1978, Faber and Faber, 1980

The Rattle Bag: An Anthology of Poetry, selected by Seamus Heaney and Ted Hughes, Faber and Faber, 1982

Sweeney Astray, Faber and Faber, 1984

Station Island, Faber and Faber, 1984

The Haw Lantern, Faber and Faber, 1987

The Government of the Tongue: The 1986 T.S. Eliot Memorial Lectures and Other Critical Writings, Faber and Faber, 1988

The Cure at Troy: A Version of Sophocles' Philoctetes, Faber and Faber, 1990

New Selected Poems 1966–1987, Faber and Faber, 1990

Seeing Things, Faber and Faber, 1991

Jan Kochanowski: Laments, translated by Seamus Heaney and Stanislaw Baranczak, Faber and Faber, 1995

The Redress of Poetry: Oxford Lectures, Faber and Faber, 1995

The Spirit Level, Faber and Faber, 1996

The School Bag, selected by Seamus Heaney and Ted Hughes, Faber and Faber, 1997

Opened Ground 1966–1996, Faber and Faber, 1998

Beowulf, Faber and Faber, 2000

Β ACKGROUND READING

R.F. Foster, *The Oxford Illustrated History of Ireland*, Oxford, 1990

Terence Brown, *Ireland: A Social and Cultural History 1922–1985*, Fontana, 1985

A.T.Q. Stewart, *The Narrow Ground: Patterns of Ulster History*, Faber and Faber, 1977

A. Norman Jeffares, *Anglo-Irish Literature*, Macmillan, 1982

Edna Longley, *The Living Stream: Literature and Revisionism in Ireland*, Bloodaxe, 1994

P.V. Glob, *The Bog People: Iron-Age Man Preserved*, Faber and Faber, 1969

Β OOKS ON SEAMUS HEANEY

Blake Morrison, *Seamus Heaney*, Methuen, 1982

Straightforward account of Seamus Heaney's first five collections

Ronald Tamplin, *Seamus Heaney*, Open University, 1989

Guide, designed for students, to poems up to *The Haw Lantern*

Tony Curtis, ed., *The Art of Seamus Heaney*, Poetry Wales, 1994
(revised, 3rd edition)
> Collection of essays by variety of critics on Seamus Heaney's poetry and prose

Elmer Andrews, ed., *Seamus Heaney: A Collection of Critical Essays*,
Macmillan, 1992
> Another selection of essays on Seamus Heaney

Michael Parker, *Seamus Heaney: The Making of the Poet*, Macmillan,
1993
> Solid account of Seamus Heaney's career with a wealth of helpful biographical
> information

Henry Hart, *Seamus Heaney: Poet of Contrary Progress*, Syracuse
University Press, 1992
> Sophisticated, quite difficult exploration of Seamus Heaney

Bernard O'Donoghue, *Seamus Heaney and the Language of Poetry*,
Harvester Wheatsheaf, 1994
> A primarily linguistic approach to Seamus Heaney's poetry. Informative on the
> Irish tradition

Michael Allen, ed., *Seamus Heaney: Contemporary Critical Essays*,
Macmillan, 1997
> Includes some essays hostile to Seamus Heaney or challenging his reputation.
> Some heavily theoretical essays

Elmer Andrews, ed., *The Poetry of Seamus Heaney*, Icon Books, 1998
> A guide to the critical reception of Seamus Heaney's work. Incorporates substantial
> quotations from a variety of critical approaches including such writers as John
> Carey, Desmond Fennell, Clair Wills and Elizabeth Butler Cullingford

Neil Corcoran, *The Poetry of Seamus Heaney*, Faber and Faber, 1998
> Robust readings of individual poems and useful biographical detail

Helen Vendler, *Soul Says: On Recent Poetry*, The Belknap Press of
Harvard University Press, 1995
> Contains three illuminating essays on Seamus Heaney alongside essays on other
> contemporary poets writing in English

Helen Vendler, *Seamus Heaney*, HarperCollins, 1998

Events in Ireland	Author's life	Literary events
1912-13 Tension mounts in Ireland; Protestant military groups in the North and Catholic groups across Ireland are established and arm themselves		
1914 The Irish Home Rule Bill, which grants an independent parliament to Ireland, passes, though enactment is delayed until 1920		**1914** James Joyce, *Dubliners;* W.B. Yeats, *Responsibilities*
1914-18 First World War; progress on Home Rule suspended because of the War		
1916 Easter Rebellion in Dublin, in which Irish nationalist forces take control of the city centre before being forced to surrender by British troops (April 24–9)		**1916** James Joyce, *A Portrait of the Artist as a Young Man*
		1918 First publication of the poems of Gerard Manley Hopkins (died 1889)
1920 Government of Ireland Act establishes six of the nine counties of Ulster as the province of Northern Ireland and grants independent parliaments to both Ireland and Northern Ireland		
1920-1 Armed struggle between Irish nationalist groups and British Army; introduction of Black and Tans		
1921 Anglo-Irish Treaty is signed, which ends the Irish War of Independence and grants limited freedom to Ireland (December 6)		
1922 The Irish Free State is established, ending the Irish Revolution (December 6)		**1922** James Joyce, *Ulysses;* T.S. Eliot, *The Waste Land;* Osip Mandelstam, *Tristia*

Events in Ireland	Author's life	Literary events
1922-3 Irish Civil War breaks out between the Free State government and Irish nationalists opposed to the Anglo-Irish Treaty and a partitioned Ireland		
		1923 Sean O'Casey, *Shadow of a Gunman*
1925 Boundary Commission collapses and partition of Ireland confirmed		**1925** Hugh MacDiarmid, *Sangschaw*
		1926 Sean O'Casey, *The Plough and the Stars;* Hugh MacDiarmid, *A Drunk Man Looks at the Thistle*
		1928 Robert Frost, *West Running Brook;* W.B. Yeats, *The Tower*
1929 Proportional representation abolished in Northern Irish parliamentary elections		**1929** Louis MacNeice, *Blind Fireworks*
		1932 T.S. Eliot, *Sweeney Agonistes;* Boris Pasternak, *Second Birth*
		1933 D.H. Lawrence, *Last Poems*
		1935 T.S. Eliot, *Murder in the Cathedral*
1936 IRA proscribed by de Valera in the Free State		**1936** Dylan Thomas, *Twenty-five Poems;* Patrick Kavanagh, *Ploughman and Other Poems;* W.H. Auden, *Look, Stranger!*
1937 Eire (formerly Irish Free State) becomes an independent member of the British Commonwealth		**1937** Stevie Smith, *A Good Time Was Had by All;* Wallace Stevens, *The Man with the Blue Guitar*
1939 IRA bombing campaign in Britain	**1939** Born at Mossbawn, County Derry, Northern Ireland	**1939** James Joyce, *Finnegans Wake;* Louis MacNeice, *Autumn Journal;*

Events in Ireland	Author's life	Literary events
1939-45 Second World War; Eire declares itself neutral; German air raids on Belfast		
		1941 Theodore Roethke, *Open House*
		1942 Patrick Kavanagh, *The Great Hunger*
		1943 T.S. Eliot, *Four Quartets*
		1946 Dylan Thomas, *Deaths and Entrances*
		1948 W.H. Auden, *The Age of Anxiety*
1949 The Republic of Ireland becomes an independent state, separate from the British Commonwealth		**1949** Ezra Pound, *Pisan Cantos;* Edwin Muir, *The Labyrinth;* Louis MacNeice, *Collected Poems 1925-48*
		1952 Samuel Beckett, *Waiting for Godot;* Philip Larkin, *The Less Deceived*
		1953 Czeslaw Milosz, *The Captive Mind*
		1955 Elizabeth Bishop, *North and South – A Cold Spring*
1956-62 IRA campaign in North		**1956** Edwin Muir, *One Foot in Eden*
	1957 Goes to Belfast to study Literature at Queen's University	**1957** Ted Hughes, *The Hawk in the Rain;* Stevie Smith, *Not Waving But Drowning*
		1958 Boris Pasternak, *Doctor Zhivago;* Brendan Behan, *The Hostage*

Events in Ireland	Author's life	Literary events
		1959 Robert Lowell, *Life Studies*
		1960 Sylvia Plath, *The Colossus*
		1962 Anna Akhmatova, *Poem Without a Hero;* Czeslaw Milosz, *King Popiel and Other Poems;* Hugh MacDiarmid, *Collected Poems;* A Alvarez, *The New Poetry*
1964 First meetings of heads of government of Northern Ireland and the Republic		**1964** Brian Friel, *Philadelphia, Here I Come!;* Robert Lowell, *For the Union Dead;* Anna Akhmatova, *Requiem;* Philip Larkin, *The Whitsun Weddings*
	1965 Marries Marie Devlin	**1965** Sylvia Plath, *Ariel*
	1966 *Death of a Naturalist*	**1966** Theodore Roethke, *Collected Poems*
		1967 Miroslav Holub, *Selected Poems*
1968 First Civil Rights March		**1968** Czeslaw Milosz, *Native Realm;* Zbigniew Herbert, *Selected Poems;* Derek Mahon, *Night Crossing;* John Hewitt, *Collected Poems 1932-67*
1969 Outbreak of sectarian and political conflict, N Ireland; British troops sent to protect Catholics	**1969** *Door into the Dark;* involved in Civil Rights Movement	**1969** Michael Longley, *No Continuing City;* Douglas Dunn, *Terry Street*
		1970 Nadezhda Mandelstam, *Hope Against Hope;* Ted Hughes, *Crow*
1971 Internment (imprisonment without trial) is introduced in Northern Ireland to combat terrorism	**1971** Lectures at University of California, Berkeley	**1971** Geoffrey Hill, *Mercian Hymns*

Events in Ireland	Author's life	Literary events
1972 'Bloody Sunday' – British troops shoot and kill 13 unarmed protesters in Londonderry; 'Bloody Friday' – IRA detonates a number of bombs in Belfast, killing 9 civilians; Parliament of Northern Ireland suspended and British impose direct rule over the province	**1972** Moves to Glanmore, County Wicklow, Republic of Ireland; *Wintering out;* works as lecturer; works as freelance writer	**1972** Ted Hughes, *Selected Poems;* Sylvia Plath, *Winter Trees;* Nadezhda Mandelstam, *Hope Abandoned*
1972-5 Troops enter the Bogside; Sunningdale Agreement on power sharing; unionist strikes bring down Executive and direct rule reimposed; the Birmingham and Guildford pub bombings		**1973** Robert Lowell, *The Dolphin;* Derek Walcott, *Another Life;* Joseph Brodsky, *Selected Poems;* R.S. Thomas, *Selected Poems 1946-68*
		1974 Philip Larkin, *High Windows*
	1975 *North*	
1976 Two women from Belfast, Mairead Corrigan and Betty Williams, receive the Nobel Peace Prize for their work to reconcile religious communities in Northern Ireland; British Ambassador in Dublin killed		**1976** Ted Hughes, *Season Songs;* Elizabeth Bishop, *Geography III*
1976-80 Foundation of the Peace People; Shankill Butchers jailed; death of Mountbatten; 12 civilians killed by Provisional IRA bomb in restaurant and 8 soldiers killed in ambush at Warrenpoint; Margaret Thatcher takes power in London		**1977** Sorley MacLean, *Reothairt is Contraigh (Spring Tide and Neap Tide: Selected Poems 1932-72);* John Ashbery, *Self-Portrait in a Convex Mirror*
		1978 Czeslaw Milosz, *Bells in Winter*

Events in Ireland	Author's life	Literary events
	1979 *Field Work*	1979 Ted Hughes, *Moortown;* Brian Friel, *Aristocrats;* Derek Walcott, *The Star-Apple Kingdom*
1980-1 IRA prisoners stage hunger strikes; ten die; riots N Ireland	1980 *Preoccupations;* becomes director in Field Day Company	1980 Joseph Brodsky, *A Part of Speech;* Paul Muldoon, *Why Brownlee Left;* Brian Friel, *Translations*
1981-4 Supergrass trials; Maze escape; bombing campaign in Britain; Margaret Thatcher escapes death in Brighton bomb		1981 Seán Ó Tuama and Thomas Kinsella, *An Duanaire (1600-1900: Poems of the Dispossessed)*
	1982-96 Professor at University of Harvard, USA for half of each year	1982 Derek Mahon, *The Hunt by Night;* Maedbh McGuckian, *The Flower Master*
	1983 *Sweeney Astray*	1983 Tom Paulin, *The Liberty Tree;* Paul Muldoon, *Quoaof*
	1984 *Station Island*	
1985-7 Anglo-Irish Agreement gives Dublin a role in the north; unionist opposition; 'shoot to kill' inquiry; the Enniskillen massacre		1985 Norman MacCaig, *Collected Poems;* Douglas Dunn, *Elegies*
	1986 Delivers T.S. Eliot Memorial Lectures	1986 Joseph Brodsky, *History of the Twentieth Century*
	1987 *The Haw Lantern*	1987 Marin Sorescu, *The Biggest Egg in the World*
1988-9 SAS kills IRA members in Gibraltar; Milltown cemetry deaths; the broadcasting ban; UK-Republic extradition rows; Guildford Four released	1988 *The Government of the Tongue*	

Events in Ireland	Author's life	Literary events
	1989-94 Chair of Poetry at Oxford University	
	1990 The Cure at Troy is produced	1990 Brian Friel, Dancing at Lughnasa; Derek Walcott, Omeros; Nuala Ni Dhomhnaill, Pharaoh's Daughter
	1991 Seeing Things	1991 Les Murray, Collected Poems
		1992 Tony Harrison, The Gaze of the Gorgon
1993 Downing Street Declaration, which establishes a framework for peace negotiations, is issued by British and Irish prime ministers		
1994 IRA calls unconditional cease-fire (August 31)		1994 Brian Friel, Molly Sweeney
	1995 The Redress of Poetry; awarded Nobel Prize for Literature	1995 Joseph Brodsky, On Grief and Reason
1996 IRA ends cease-fire by bombing London's Docklands district, injuring over 100 (February 9)	1996 The Spirit Level	
1998 Good Friday agreement signed by main groups of Unionists and Nationalists; Omagh bombing kills 29 civilians; Nobel Peace prize awarded to John Hume (Nationalist) and David Trimble (Unionist)	1998 Opened Ground	1998 Ted Hughes, Birthday Letters
	1999 Beowulf (translation)	

Aisling (Irish for dream or vision) a traditional type of poem in Irish, written as a love poem but the loved one is a female embodiment of Ireland. It expresses a longing for an independent Ireland

alliteration a sequence of repeated consonantal sounds in a stretch of language. The matching consonants are usually at the beginning of words or stressed syllables. It is common in poetry and prose, and is one of the most easily identifiable figures of speech

anapaest a trisyllabic metrical foot consisting of two unstressed syllables followed by a stressed syllable: ti-ti-tum

assonance the use of the same vowel sounds with different consonants in successive words or stressed syllables e.g. nation and traitor

Celtic Twilight in 1893 W.B. Yeats published a collection of stories of the supernatural based on orally transmitted accounts collected by him in the west of Ireland. The title *The Celtic Twilight* came to be employed of a dreamy, quaint, otherworldly, rural dimension in Ireland where fairies and magic are commonplace. It is also used to describe the literature, mainly at the turn of the century, involved in this dimension

couplet a pair of consecutively rhyming lines

dialect a form of language spoken in a particular geographical area, or by members of a particular social class or occupational group, distinguished by its vocabulary, grammar and pronunciation

diction the choice of words in a work of literature – the kind of vocabulary used

dinnshenchas (Irish for love of place) a traditional piece of writing in which local places, their names and their lore are celebrated

dramatic voice see persona

elegy a poem of lamentation, concentrating on the death of a single person

foot in order to work out the metre of a line of verse, it is necessary to divide it into 'feet', which are certain fixed combinations of weakly and strongly stressed syllables into which the line is divided e.g. iamb

free verse verse released from the convention of metre with its regular pattern of stresses and lengths. It is printed in broken-up lines like verse (not continuously like prose) and may be rhythmical

grammar the way words combine to form sentences; see syntax

half-rhyme an imperfect rhyme

iamb the commonest metrical foot in English verse – consisting of a weak stress followed by a strong stress e.g. ti-tum

image, imagery all the words which refer to objects and qualities which appeal to the senses and feelings; see also metaphor and simile

irony saying one thing while you mean another

metaphor a figure of speech in which a word or phrase is applied to an object or action that it does not literally denote in order to imply a resemblance

metre the rhythmic and regular arrangement of words and syllables

myth myths are stories, usually concerning super-humans or gods, which are related to accompany or explain religious beliefs. In recent criticism the word tends to lose its connections with religion and is used to describe the complete range of systems and signs by which a society expresses its cultural values

New Criticism a major critical movement that recommended that a poem must be studied as a poem and not as a piece of biographical or sociological evidence, or literary-historical material, or as a demonstration of a psychological theory of literature, or for any other reason. Close reading of texts became the only legitimate critical procedure seeing the work as a linguistic structure

octave a stanza of eight lines

parable a short narrative devised so as to give a clear demonstration of a moral or lesson

pathos moments in works of art which evoke strong feelings of pity and sorrow

persona the point of view or characteristics of the narrator

quatrain a stanza of four lines

rhyme chiming or matching sounds which create a very clearly audible sense of pattern

rhythm the chief element of rhythm is the variation in levels of stress accorded to the syllables

sestet a stanza of six lines

simile a figure of speech in which one thing is explicitly said to be like another; similes always contain the words 'like' or 'as'

sonnet poem of fourteen lines, usually of iambic pentameter, with a complicated rhyme scheme. Some sonnets divide into three quatrains and a final couplet; some divide into an octave (eight lines) and a sestet (six lines)

stanza a unit of several lines of verse; a repeated group of lines of verse

stress in any word of more than one syllable, more emphasis or loudness will be given to one of the syllables in comparison with the others. More significant words, such as nouns and verbs, tend to bear strong stress

syntax the arrangement of words in their appropriate forms and proper order, in order to achieve meaning

terza rima verse form consisting of three-line units in which the first and third lines rhyme and the second line provides the rhyme sound for the first and third lines of the following unit. In English poetry, the lines usually contain ten syllables or five main stresses. There are several less strict variations on this basic scheme

triplets a stanza of three similar lines

verse commonly refers to poetry in general, especially to denote metrical writing rather than prose

Author of this note

Alasdair Macrae graduated from the University of Edinburgh. He taught in the University of Khartoum before becoming a lecturer and later Senior Lecturer at the University of Stirling. He has published widely on modern poetry, including *W.B. Yeats: A Literary Life*.

York Notes Advanced (£3.99 each)

Margaret Atwood
Cat's Eye

Margaret Atwood
The Handmaid's Tale

Jane Austen
Mansfield Park

Jane Austen
Persuasion

Jane Austen
Pride and Prejudice

Alan Bennett
Talking Heads

William Blake
Songs of Innocence and of Experience

Charlotte Brontë
Jane Eyre

Emily Brontë
Wuthering Heights

Angela Carter
Nights at the Circus

Geoffrey Chaucer
The Franklin's Prologue and Tale

Geoffrey Chaucer
The Miller's Prologue and Tale

Geoffrey Chaucer
Prologue To the Canterbury Tales

Geoffrey Chaucer
The Wife of Bath's Prologue and Tale

Samuel Taylor Coleridge
Selected Poems

Joseph Conrad
Heart of Darkness

Daniel Defoe
Moll Flanders

Charles Dickens
Great Expectations

Charles Dickens
Hard Times

Emily Dickinson
Selected Poems

John Donne
Selected Poems

Carol Ann Duffy
Selected Poems

George Eliot
Middlemarch

George Eliot
The Mill on the Floss

T.S. Eliot
Selected Poems

F. Scott Fitzgerald
The Great Gatsby

E.M. Forster
A Passage to India

Brian Friel
Translations

Thomas Hardy
The Mayor of Casterbridge

Thomas Hardy
The Return of the Native

Thomas Hardy
Selected Poems

Thomas Hardy
Tess of the d'Urbervilles

Seamus Heaney
Selected Poems from Opened Ground

Nathaniel Hawthorne
The Scarlet Letter

Kazuo Ishiguro
The Remains of the Day

Ben Jonson
The Alchemist

James Joyce
Dubliners

John Keats
Selected Poems

Christopher Marlowe
Doctor Faustus

Arthur Miller
Death of a Salesman

John Milton
Paradise Lost Books I & II

Toni Morrison
Beloved

Alexander Pope
Rape of the Lock and other poems

William Shakespeare
Antony and Cleopatra

William Shakespeare
As You Like It

William Shakespeare
Hamlet

William Shakespeare
King Lear

William Shakespeare
Measure for Measure

William Shakespeare
The Merchant of Venice

William Shakespeare
A Midsummer Night's Dream

William Shakespeare
Much Ado About Nothing

William Shakespeare
Othello

William Shakespeare
Richard II

William Shakespeare
Romeo and Juliet

William Shakespeare
The Taming of the Shrew

William Shakespeare
The Tempest

William Shakespeare
The Winter's Tale

George Bernard Shaw
Saint Joan

Mary Shelley
Frankenstein

Alice Walker
The Color Purple

Oscar Wilde
The Importance of Being Earnest

Tennessee Williams
A Streetcar Named Desire

John Webster
The Duchess of Malfi

Virginia Woolf
To the Lighthouse

W.B. Yeats
Selected Poems

GCSE and equivalent levels (£3.50 each)

Maya Angelou
I Know Why the Caged Bird Sings

Jane Austen
Pride and Prejudice

Alan Ayckbourn
Absent Friends

Elizabeth Barrett Browning
Selected Poems

Robert Bolt
A Man for All Seasons

Harold Brighouse
Hobson's Choice

Charlotte Brontë
Jane Eyre

Emily Brontë
Wuthering Heights

Shelagh Delaney
A Taste of Honey

Charles Dickens
David Copperfield

Charles Dickens
Great Expectations

Charles Dickens
Hard Times

Charles Dickens
Oliver Twist

Roddy Doyle
Paddy Clarke Ha Ha Ha

George Eliot
Silas Marner

George Eliot
The Mill on the Floss

William Golding
Lord of the Flies

Oliver Goldsmith
She Stoops To Conquer

Willis Hall
The Long and the Short and the Tall

Thomas Hardy
Far from the Madding Crowd

Thomas Hardy
The Mayor of Casterbridge

Thomas Hardy
Tess of the d'Urbervilles

Thomas Hardy
The Withered Arm and other Wessex Tales

L.P. Hartley
The Go-Between

Seamus Heaney
Selected Poems

Susan Hill
I'm the King of the Castle

Barry Hines
A Kestrel for a Knave

Louise Lawrence
Children of the Dust

Harper Lee
To Kill a Mockingbird

Laurie Lee
Cider with Rosie

Arthur Miller
The Crucible

Arthur Miller
A View from the Bridge

Robert O'Brien
Z for Zachariah

Frank O'Connor
My Oedipus Complex and Other Stories

George Orwell
Animal Farm

J.B. Priestley
An Inspector Calls

Willy Russell
Educating Rita

Willy Russell
Our Day Out

J.D. Salinger
The Catcher in the Rye

William Shakespeare
Henry IV Part 1

William Shakespeare
Henry V

William Shakespeare
Julius Caesar

William Shakespeare
Macbeth

William Shakespeare
The Merchant of Venice

William Shakespeare
A Midsummer Night's Dream

William Shakespeare
Much Ado About Nothing

William Shakespeare
Romeo and Juliet

William Shakespeare
The Tempest

William Shakespeare
Twelfth Night

George Bernard Shaw
Pygmalion

Mary Shelley
Frankenstein

R.C. Sherriff
Journey's End

Rukshana Smith
Salt on the Snow

John Steinbeck
Of Mice and Men

Robert Louis Stevenson
Dr Jekyll and Mr Hyde

Jonathan Swift
Gulliver's Travels

Robert Swindells
Daz 4 Zoe

Mildred D. Taylor
Roll of Thunder, Hear My Cry

Mark Twain
Huckleberry Finn

James Watson
Talking in Whispers

William Wordsworth
Selected Poems

A Choice of Poets

Mystery Stories of the Nineteenth Century including The Signalman

Nineteenth Century Short Stories

Poetry of the First World War

Six Women Poets

Chinua Achebe
Things Fall Apart

Jane Austen
Emma

Jane Austen
Northanger Abbey

Jane Austen
Sense and Sensibility

Samuel Beckett
Waiting for Godot and
Endgame

Louis de Bernières
Captain Corelli's Mandolin

Charlotte Brontë
Villette

Geoffrey Chaucer
The Merchant's Tale

Geoffrey Chaucer
The Nun's Priest's Tale

Caryl Churchill
Top Girls and *Cloud Nine*

Charles Dickens
Bleak House

T.S. Eliot
The Waste Land

Henry Fielding
Joseph Andrews

Anne Frank
The Diary of Anne Frank

Thomas Hardy
Jude the Obscure

Homer
The Iliad

Homer
The Odyssey

Henrik Ibsen
The Doll's House and *Ghosts*

Ben Jonson
Volpone

James Joyce
*A Portrait of the Artist as a
Young Man*

Philip Larkin
Selected Poems

Aldous Huxley
Brave New World

D.H. Lawrence
Selected Poems

Christopher Marlowe
Edward II

John Milton
Paradise Lost Bks IV & IX

Thomas More
Utopia

George Orwell
Nineteen Eighty-four

Sylvia Plath
Selected Poems

J.B. Priestley
When We Are Married

Jean Rhys
Wide Sargasso Sea

William Shakespeare
As You Like It

William Shakespeare
Coriolanus

William Shakespeare
Henry IV Pt I

Wliiam Shakespeare
Henry IV Part II

William Shakespeare
Henry V

William Shakespeare
Julius Caesar

William Shakespeare
Macbeth

William Shakespeare
Richard III

William Shakespeare
Sonnets

William Shakespeare
Twelfth Night

Tom Stoppard
Arcadia and *Rosencrantz and
Guildenstern are Dead*

Jonathan Swift
*Gulliver's Travels and A Modest
Proposal*

Alfred, Lord Tennyson
Selected Poems

Virgil
The Aeneid

Edith Wharton
Ethan Frome

Jeanette Winterson
*Oranges are Not the Only
Fruit*

Tennessee Williams
Cat on a Hot Tin Roof

Virginia Woolf
Mrs Dalloway

Metaphysical Poets

NOTES

NOTES

NOTES